The THINK Series

THINK about
Immigration

9

THINK *about*
Immigration

Social Diversity in the U.S.

by Leon F. Bouvier
The THINK Series

Walker and Company
720 Fifth Avenue.
New York City, NY

First published in the United States of America in 1988 by the Walker Publishing Company, Inc.

Published simultaneously in Canada by Thomas Allen & Son Canada, Limited, Markham, Ontario.

Library of Congress Cataloging-in-Publication Data

Bouvier, Leon F.
  Think about immigration.

  (The Think series)
  Bibliography: p.
  Includes index.
  Summary: Discusses immigration examining some of the causes that motivate people to immigrate and how the arrival of new people affects individuals and the nation as a whole.
    1. Immigrants—United States—History—Juvenile literature. [1. Emigration and immigration] I. Title.
II. Series.
JV6450.B68   1988   325.73   87-23012
ISBN 0-8027-6755-9
ISBN 0-8027-6756-7 (pbk.)

Printed in the United States of America

10 9 8 7 6 5 4 3 2 1

The THINK Series' Editors: William N. Thorndike Jr.,
Ramsey R. Walker

Stylistic editor: Mary Jo Willy
Assistant stylistic editor: Mary Pavlik
Fact checker: Catherine Monk
Reading consultants: Anne-Marie Longo, Paula Sable

Jacket design: Joyce C. Weston
Text design: Joyce C. Weston
Photo research: Diane Hamilton
Graphs: Jill Thompson
Jacket illustration: Tom Hughes
Text illustrations: Jeff Danziger
Appendix A written by J.B. Schramm

The editors would like to thank the many teachers, librarians,
and students that assisted in putting together the THINK
Series. It would be impossible to thank everybody; however,
we would especially like to thank the following people: John
Buckey, Betty Carter, Jim Davis, Mike Hartoonian, Tedd Levy,
David Mallery, Mike Printz, Bill Polk, Ellen Ramsey.

Author's Acknowledgment

I take this opportunity to thank my spouse, Terri. Without her help this book would never have been completed.

Figures 1, 3, 9, 13, 14, 17, 19, 20, 21 courtesy of the Library of Congress; Figure 4 courtesy of the U.S. Navy; Figures 5, 18, 25 Copyright the Washington Post; reprinted by permission of the D.C. Public Library.

CONTENTS

1 Introduction

What is the significance of immigration to you?

What is the difference between emigration and immigration?

Why do people immigrate?

What are the different types of immigration?

Immigration affects every one of you. In fact, it touches all people, everywhere. You are probably descended from immigrants. Perhaps *you* immigrated to the United States, alone or with other members of your family. Perhaps you are one of those who made the journey across international borders to reach a new place to live.

The movement, or migration, of many people changes the places they leave and the places where they decide to resettle. The United States continues to change because of the immigration of people from other countries.

This chapter discusses the effects of immigration on you. But first, it defines the difference between migration and immigration. It tells you about some of the causes that motivate people to immigrate. And it ends with a discussion of the results of immigration—how the arrival of new people affects you individually and the nation as a whole.

Most of you will move at least once during your lifetime, even if it is just a few blocks away. Some of you will move to a new neighborhood across town. For others, the move will be to a new state. Some of you will take up residence in a new country—a country with different laws and strange customs for you to learn.

However it is made, the decision to move is a difficult one for most people. Moving is not easy. Imagine the experience of the hundreds of thousands of Europeans who decided to move to the United States in the early 1900s. First, they said goodbye to everyone they knew and everything that was familiar to them. Then they traveled to a port city, booked passage on a ship, and left. Their boat arrived at Ellis Island in the New York City harbor after a dangerous and uncomfortable journey. The travelers were uncertain whether they would be allowed to enter the United States.

First of all, the immigrants had to prove that they had enough money to take care of themselves, or they were refused admittance to the U.S. Yet most of them had to come to the U.S. because of the poverty they experienced in their homeland. Most lacked the money necessary to live comfortably, and they had little chance of earning enough to live comfortably in the future.

If arriving passengers were sick or appeared unhealthy they were turned away. Yet years of not having enough to eat combined with the hard sea voyage they had just endured caused many of them to be ill on arrival.

Figure 1   An immigrant family on their way to New York City,
1905.

Imagine the disappointment of those who were rejected by U.S. immigration authorities. For many, moving to America was the only hope they had for a better future. If they were turned away, they faced another difficult trip across the Atlantic Ocean. The trip back home could last a month and result in a disappointment shared by other family members.

If the immigrant gained entrance to the U.S., other difficulties lay ahead. Where to work? How to live? Who would understand their language, their customs? Who would understand their eating habits? Who would appreciate their religious and social practices? Who would teach them how to get along in the United States?

These same difficulties were faced by other immigrants during other periods of immigration. They were shared by those brave and sometimes desperate people who moved here from Africa, Asia, Central and South America. They were shared by all who arrived, whether by sea, air, or across land.

Each of you has an interesting story to tell about a

Figure 2   New immigrants were faced with many uncertainties when they arrived in the United States.

relative, a friend, or an ancestor who made such a journey. Perhaps *you* immigrated to the United States.

All of these immigration stories—taken as a whole—reveal the reasons for the rich cultural diversity of the United States population. How do the immigrants themselves feel? Henry Grunwald, editor-in-chief of *Time* and an immigrant to the U.S. from Austria, summed it up: "Every immigrant leads a double life. Every immigrant has a double vision and a double identity, being suspended between an old and a new home, an old and a new self." This feeling probably never ends for those of you who are immigrants yourselves.

You should understand the difference in meaning between migration and immigration. Migration is simply the movement from one place to another. Only those persons who leave one country to take up residence in another are called immigrants.

Immigration, then, is the act of leaving one's country to settle in another country. Webster's Dictionary defines an immigrant as "a person who came to a country to take up permanent residence."

More specifically, the act of leaving one's native country is called emigration. The act of entering another country is called immigration. Each immigrant to the United States has emigrated from some other country. For example, Patrick Ewing, the great basketball star who joined the New York Knicks after playing at Georgetown University, was born in Jamaica. He migrated to the United States as a teenager. Ewing is an **emigrant** from Jamaica; he is an **immigrant** to the United States.

Why would someone like Patrick Ewing make the

Figure 3   A Norwegian woman bidding her family farewell before leaving for the United States.

decision to move so far from his native land and culture? There are many reasons.

REASONS FOR IMMIGRATION

Most people who move do so for economic reasons. They want a better life. They firmly believe that immigrating to another country will give them the opportunity to achieve that better life.

Economic motives propel the Haitian who risks his life in a leaky boat to reach the Florida coastline. Economics cause others to move, like the Filipino nurse who left her home to apply for a better nursing job in a California hospital. Mexican farm laborers cross the borders of California and Texas to earn more money than they are able to earn in their country's job market.

There are many other, noneconomic reasons for moving. Political refugees move because they fear for their lives. Some persons simply want to live in the free atmosphere that is enjoyed by Americans. Mikhail Baryshnikov defected from the Soviet Union and his honored position in the Kirov Ballet because he wanted artistic freedom. He lived in a rigid society, and he wanted independence. He enjoyed a high standard of living in the Soviet Union. Moreover, he was famous. He was allowed to travel all over the world. But it was not enough. Now he is artistic director of the American Ballet Theater. He has thrived in the United States and has stated publicly that he will never return to the Soviet Union.

Historically, many persons were forced to immigrate to the United States. Boatload after boatload of Africans were brought to the U.S. against their will. They were enslaved as a source of free labor for plantation owners in the southern colonies. The original motivation behind slavery was economic. Cotton and tobacco were major cash crops in the South. Planting and harvesting them required much manual labor. Plantation owners purchased slaves, who were forced to perform this labor. Slavery became the first civil rights issue and the source of many debates. President Abraham Lincoln declared the abolition of slavery in 1863, with the issuance of the Emancipation Proclamation. Civil War broke out the same year. It was not until the end of the war, in 1865, that the abolition of slavery was enforced throughout the nation. An unfortunate chapter in American history was closed.

Family reunification is another reason people move. Often, young family members are the first to decide to immigrate. Later, their aging parents might join them. Sometimes brothers, sisters, or cousins decide to follow. Even in these situations, the underlying cause is often economic. Often, relatives want to follow the path laid by the first immigrants in a family. The first immigrants have often found good jobs and are enjoying the healthy economic environment of the United States. Their success makes others in the family want to follow.

The economic rewards of immigration can be different for different persons. For some, economic survival means the difference between living and dying. Ethiopians and others who emigrate from a land where crops, livestock, and people are dying may find new jobs when they arrive in the United States. More important, they find an abundance of food to purchase with the money they earn.

Ultimately, the reasons for moving and immigrating can be defined as "push" or "pull" reasons. This is true of economic and noneconomic reasons.

If survival is at stake, a person is pushed to move. The push can result from the potential for starvation, or from the fear of political terrorism or death. Today, many Ethiopian farmers run from certain starvation. Many Central Americans flee political terrorism.

In other instances, conditions are not intolerable at home. The potential immigrant could stay home and survive. However, he hears that life is better in the United States. He is attracted, or pulled, by the possibility of finding that better life. An example of this pull to immigrate is the Mexico City citizen who hears about better jobs in Los Angeles and crosses the border to try his fortune.

You will be able to put other reasons for immigration into either push or pull categories.

KINDS OF IMMIGRATION

In the United States, there are four types of immigration: legal, refugee, forced, and illegal. A discussion of each type follows.

Most people who come to live in the United States are **legal immigrants.** Historically, most immigrants have been from this group. After deciding to leave their homeland, they went to the United States Embassy in their country for a permanent visa to come to the United States. When the visa was granted, they made the trip. Upon arrival, they applied for permanent residence. This was an important step because it allowed them to apply legally for jobs. After residing in the United States for five years, they could apply for citizenship. Most became American citizens, just like millions who were born here and achieved their citizenship by right of birth.

Most legal immigrants responded to "pull" factors. They made a voluntary decision to move. They decided that the place to which they were moving was more attractive than the place they were leaving.

The second type of immigration is that undertaken by **refugees.** The United Nations has defined refugees as "persons suffering persecution because of political opinion, membership in a particular social group, race, ethnicity, or religion." Refugees have generally left their homeland because they feared for their lives. The contemporary world is dotted with refugee settlements.

Best estimates are that 15 million refugees are scattered around the world.

Today, the United States accepts over one hundred thousand refugees every year. In 1974 and 1975, during the closing days of the Vietnam War, millions left southeast Asia and fled to the United States. Some left because they had helped the American forces. Others left simply because they feared their lives were in danger due to the imminent takeover of South Vietnam by the Communist regime from the north.

Refugees are pushed from their homeland. They would rather stay where they are. However, they realize that to remain in their homeland would result in starvation, imprisonment, or death.

Refugees are not a new phenomenon. Many early American settlers were refugees from religious and political persecution in Europe. Some were forced to flee Great Britain because of their refusal to accept the religious beliefs of their king. Other early Americans left Germany because their political opinions were considered dangerous.

A third type of immigration is forced, or involuntary, immigration. Forced **immigrants** were granted

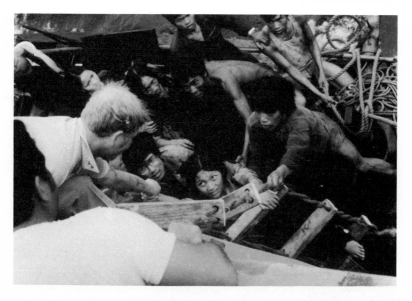

Figure 4   Vietnamese refugees being taken aboard an American ship in the South China Sea, 1981.

no choice in the matter of their movement from their homeland to a new country. Forced immigration has resulted in the enslavement of millions of human beings throughout history.

United States history provides a dramatic example of forced immigration—the capture and selling of millions of African natives as a source of slave labor in the United States. Millions of Africans entered the U.S. in this manner. It represents one of the largest immigration streams in history.

As stated earlier, the United States has not engaged in forced migration since around 1800. The Emancipation Proclamation of 1863 paved the way for freeing all slaves and outlawing future slavery. However, the idea, or concept, of forced migration remains a human concern.

Illegal immigrants, a fourth type, are a direct contrast to those who have gone through the legal steps necessary to move to the United States. An *illegal immigrant* is one who entered the country illegally, or one who entered legally but violated the terms of entry, remaining in the United States beyond the expiration date entered on his or her visa.

Each year, thousands of people cross the Rio Grande from Mexico in search of work. Most are Mexican citizens; however, some are from Central and South America. Some are illegal immigrants. Others enter the country legally, using temporary nonmigrant visas. The overstay their visa time limit, and attempt to hide from immigration authorities. If caught, these illegal immigrants are returned to their homeland. However, these immigrants are acting from the same motivation that compels legal immigrants. They simply seek a better life elsewhere. They have decided that the most attractive "elsewhere" is the United States.

Residence in the United States often ends abruptly for illegal immigrants, or illegal aliens, as they are usually called. At best, an illegal immigrant lives daily with the fear of being found out and deported.

Of the four types of immigration, legal immigration is the ideal way to enter the United States. It has been the chosen method for most immigrants to the United States for over two centuries. Unfortunately, it is not available to everyone who would like to come here. Many historical, contemporary, and future issues surrounding immigration arise from this important fact.

Figure 5 Captured illegal alien aboard a bus returning him to Mexico.

RELEVANCE OF IMMIGRATION

Why should you be interested in immigration? Why should it concern you? After all, you will probably always live in the United States.

First of all, you or an ancestor of yours immigrated to this country. You would probably not be sitting in your classroom today if someone in your family, sometime in the last three hundred years, had not taken a gamble on moving to the United States. Nor would most of your classmates be sitting with you.

Another reason for you to be interested in immigration is to discover how diverse your own ethnic background is. Are you descended from parents of one race, one culture, one religion? Or are you the result of the mixing and blending of more than one nationality? Perhaps you are a combination of as many as eight ethnic backgrounds, one from each of your eight great-grandparents. Whatever your parentage, your home life is affected by the ethnicity of your parents and their ancestors. Your family practices the customs it does in large part because of its particular cultural heritage. It would be interesting and fun for you to discover which customs your family practices because certain family ancestors practiced them a long time ago.

Thirdly, it is worth your while to understand just what immigration means—to the immigrant, the place the immigrant leaves, and the place the immigrant resettles in.

When a friend tells you that he or she is moving, you might not think about it much, except to wonder how much you will miss that person. Maybe the two of you walk to school together or share a hobby. If you share a particularly sad or happy memory, you will feel that part of you is leaving, too. Just imagine what happens when your experience—saying good-bye to a close friend—is shared by thousands, even millions of other people. The neighborhoods, towns, and countries that all of these people leave are changed forever. And the places they move to also change.

Finally, new settlers in your neighborhood bring their cultural heritage, their skills, and their memories with them. Ideally, they share all of these things with their new neighbors. Welcoming new persons to your neighborhood can result in a period of discovery. You have the opportunity to find out what is unique about your new neighbors' cultural heritage. Some customs may appeal to you so much that you blend them with your own. You may, for example, decide that you like a particular food your new neighbors prepare, and prepare it in your own home.

The blending of cultures is exactly how America achieved its cultural diversity, which is unique in all the world. America's success as a democracy has resulted partly from its success in accepting new citizens from around the globe. Each cultural group has made a contribution to American society.

REVIEW QUESTIONS

1. What are some of the reasons why people immigrate to the U.S.?
2. What are the difficulties that immigrants to this country face, and how do they cope with these problems?
3. What are three types of immigrants and what are the differences between them?
4. How has immigration improved or been detrimental to our society as a whole? Explain.

2 Historical Background

What are the historical patterns of immigration to the United States?

How many immigrants have come to the U.S. throughout our history?

What countries have the immigrants come from historically?

What have been the immigration characteristics of different periods in U.S. history?

What restrictive immigration laws have been passed by the U.S. government?

What is cultural diversity?

This chapter traces the development of immigration to the United States from before 1776 to today. It covers four periods: (1) Pre-1776 and the Revolutionary War; (2) **Old Immigration** from 1800 through 1881; (3) **New Immigration** from 1882 through 1964; and (4) Current Immigration from 1965 to the present.

For each period, the discussion includes the numbers of immigrants and their **countries of origin.** It relates what their arrival meant to the nation. It also describes the legislative issues that emerged as a result of the immigration. You will discover how important immigrants were to the cultural development of the United States.

PRE-1776 AND THE REVOLUTIONARY WAR

The time before the Revolutionary War is often called America's Colonial Era. Much immigration occurred before 1776, before the U.S. broke away from Great Britain. Some of you can trace your American ancestry to this period. It is easy to forget that those people were also immigrants.

President Franklin D. Roosevelt pointed to this fact in a speech he made to the Daughters of the American Revolution in the 1930s. Members of the Daughters of the American Revolution group have ancestors who came to America on the first boats from Europe. President Roosevelt addressed the DAR membership as "my fellow immigrants." Roosevelt was merely emphasizing the point that we are all immigrants, or the descendants of immigrants. It does not make any difference when we or our ancestors arrived in America; we constitute a nation of immigrants.

An exception to this statement is often noted: "except for Native Americans." But even the Native Americans' ancestors immigrated to what is now the United States. It is generally agreed that they probably came across a land bridge between Siberia and Alaska. These immigrants were Asian, and although they varied their language and culture after resettling here, they are all descendants of the Mongoloid, or Asian, branch of humankind. Very little is known about the dangerous voyages these early immigrants undertook. They moved across an entire continent to improve their lives. They were, perhaps, motivated by the same desire for an improved existence that encouraged so many others to repeat their move.

Immigration to what is now the U.S. began in earnest in the sixteenth century. Historical information is limited to those movements that began shortly after Columbus' 1492 voyage to Santo Domingo.

It is impossible to know how many early settlers came to the colonies. No immigration reports were kept. However, the first census sheds some light on immigration during this early period. When it was taken in 1790, the population of the United States totalled about four million people.

Almost all of those counted in that first census were immigrants themselves, or the children and grandchildren of immigrants. Native Americans were not counted in the first census. Most were not under the jurisdiction of the United States government. Black slaves, involuntary immigrants to the United States, were each counted as three-fifths of a person. The practice reflects the intense and unjust prejudice prevalent in the country at that time. Because the census ignored vast areas of the country that were not states at the time, many other persons were not included in the population count.

The colonial immigrants included those settlers from Great Britain and elsewhere who were the nation's founding fathers. They included the French and Spanish immigrants who settled the West, Southwest, and Midwest. They also included African immigrants brought here prior to the American Revolution.

Thus, the inhabitants of North America in 1776 were already diverse. They already represented many races, religions, and ethnic groups. They spoke different languages. In the original thirteen states, twenty percent of the settlers were not from Great Britain. This one-fifth of the population came from Ireland, France, Germany, Holland, or Denmark. In the Louisiana Territory, most immigrants were from France or Spain. In the vast, sparsely populated Southwest, settlers were likely to be Spanish or Mexican.

Some early settlers of English ancestry were unhappy about the cultural diversity that existed here. Benjamin Franklin was concerned that his beloved colony of Pennsylvania would become "Germanized." In 1751 he wrote, "This Pennsylvania will in a few years become a German colony; instead of their learning our language, we must learn theirs, or live as in a foreign country." Franklin's concerns did not turn into reality. No one was forced to learn German in order to live in Pennsylvania. However, German is still spoken almost exclusively among the Amish and Mennonite religious groups of Pennsylvania. They chose to live apart from the rest of American society in other ways, too. They did not change their lifestyles or working habits to conform to those of Americans elsewhere, who used new technology.

There were no laws that limited immigration during the Colonial Era. Before 1776, Europeans were encouraged to come here. The Spanish who settled the Southwest were welcomed.

England did not intend to populate America with its citizens. The government there discouraged its

Figure 6   An Amish man pictured with his horse and wagon. Descendants of German settlers, the Amish shun modern technology and live in the traditional manner of the eighteenth century.

citizens from emigrating to the thirteen colonies. This policy was one of the reasons the colonists decided to break ties with England.

Cultural diversity became a reality early in the settlement of this continent. Not everyone who arrived here spoke the same language, practiced the same religion, ate the same types of food, wore the same clothing. Cultural diversity sometimes led to tension, hostility, and behavior based on prejudice.

European settlers massacred thousands of Native Americans. They forced others to resettle on reservations. African slaves suffered miserably under the treatment of most white settlers.

There were bad feelings among the European settlers themselves. In the East, English colonists and other early settlers disliked and mistrusted one another. In spite of these disturbing factors, the nation survived, grew, and increased in cultural diversity.

Without the continued immigration of many people from many locations, the United States would never have become what it is today: a population rich in cultural variety. Each race, each ethnic group made unique contributions to America. Each group helped to define America. You also contribute to America's cultural diversity. You participate in the cultural benefits provided by others.

OLD IMMIGRATION: 1800–1881

After the colonies declared themselves independent from Great Britain in 1776, immigration became more important as an ingredient in the growth of the new nation. Yet the first effort to count immigrants did not begin until 1819. An act passed that year required the captain or master of a vessel arriving from abroad to deliver to the local collector of customs a list, or manifest, of all passengers taken on board.

Between the end of the Revolutionary War and 1819, about two hundred fifty thousand persons arrived in the U.S. by ship. Data collected since 1819 provides a fairly accurate count of how many legal immigrants entered the U.S.

From 1819 to 1881 10 million people immigrated

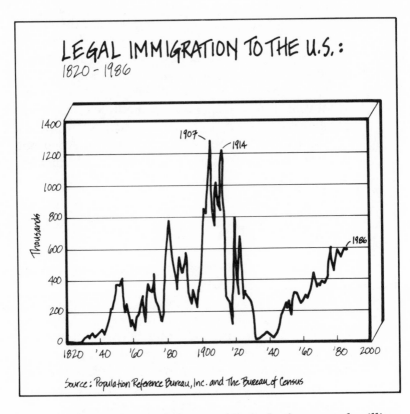

LEGAL IMMIGRATION TO THE U.S.:
1820 - 1986

Source: Population Reference Bureau, Inc. and The Bureau of Census

legally. The total does not include the several million Africans who were forced to immigrate here. Their immigration was not tracked by the U.S. government. Immigration increased decade by decade.

These new residents constituted a growing percentage of the U.S. population. By 1860, just before the start of the Civil War, one out of seven Americans was an immigrant or a child of immigrants.

In 1882, there were 50 million residents in this country. Post-Revolutionary War immigrants and their descendants outnumbered the descendants of the original colonial settlers. The United States had also expanded to the Pacific Ocean. The nation was peopled by immigrants from across the globe. East to west, the nation was dotted with settlements.

Four out of five of the people who arrived here between 1800 and 1882 came from Europe. However, some shifts in country of origin were occurring.

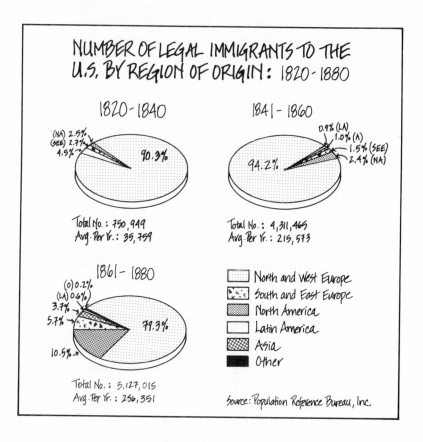

Soon after 1820, Ireland replaced the United Kingdom as the country providing the largest number of U.S. immigrants. By 1850, Germany was the immigrants' leading country of origin. Other countries of origin were France, Norway, and Sweden. Canadians of English and French ancestry also came to the U.S. Many Americans can trace their ancestors' arrival to one of these great migrations to the United States.

February 2, 1848, is the traditional date given for the arrival of the first immigrants from China. There were only three of them. Imagine how lonely they must have been in this strange country where no one spoke their language or understood their customs.

Fortunately for those three courageous settlers, forty-one thousand Chinese immigrants joined them here in the next ten years. By 1870, one hundred twenty-three thousand more had crossed the Pacific Ocean to resettle on the west coast of America. The sudden growth in Chinese immigration was caused partly by the California Gold Rush of 1848.

The Gold Rush was responsible for much of the settlement of the American West. Most prospectors did not find gold. Some of them died, like the unlucky Swiss immigrant, Paul Mathis. He was killed while protecting his gold-prospecting stake from a claim jumper. Some unsuccessful gold prospectors turned to farming and ranching, or settled new towns.

Prospectors and other new residents changed America between 1776 and 1882. Descendants of immigrants made other changes. Most U.S. citizens were still white. Most were descended from the original British colonists, at least on one side of their parentage. However, second- and third-generation

Figure 9 Cover of **Harper's Weekly** *Magazine showing newly arrived Chinese immigrants in the San Francisco Custom house, 1877.*

Americans had no memory of England or the European continent. Their collective memories began in America. They changed the customs of their parents to adapt to the physical and social climate of their new country, the United States.

These white, Anglo-Saxon Protestants were given the acronym **WASP**. The acronym was formed from the first letters of their characteristics. They were still in the majority. However, they had been joined by many Catholics from Ireland and Germany. Many people of Jewish faith had arrived by 1890. Most of them came from Germany, Poland, and Russia.

By the time of the Mexican War in 1846, the western part of the continent had been settled, mostly by Mexicans and others of Spanish origin. The addition of the Southwest to the United States at the end of the war meant that the new Spanish citizens were added to the Catholic populuation. The nation's non-white population also increased greatly with the flow of immigration from China.

During the period when these changes were occurring, Americans began showing their mixed feelings about immigration. Until then, no restrictions had been placed on anyone desiring to come here. This Open Door Policy had been in effect since George Washington's presidency.

In 1783, our government declared that all immigrants were welcome. "The bosom of America is open to receive not only the opulent and respectable stranger but the oppressed and persecuted of all nations and religions whom we shall welcome to a participation of all our rights and privileges, if by decency and propriety of conduct they appear to merit the enjoyment."

Obviously, the nation originally welcomed new immigrants. As time passed, however, feelings began to change. Some Americans became suspicious of newcomers, especially those who were different from themselves. Others thought that immigrants were taking jobs away from native-born Americans. These concerns often resulted in the formation of societies to "protect" Americans against immigrants.

On the east coast, in cities like Boston and New York, anti-Catholic and anti-Semitic (Jewish) feelings were strong. The Know Nothing political party became powerful in the 1850s, before the start of the Civil War in 1861. It attracted many Americans who were against the continued immigration of Catholics from Europe.

There was other evidence of prejudice. Many Americans of European ancestry—Protestant, Catholic, and Jewish alike—were wary of immigrants arriv-

Figure 10   Sign depicting the anti-Irish sentiments that existed in the mid-nineteenth century. This was typical of the suspicious attitudes toward new immigrants held by many Americans at the time.

ing from outside Europe. The first such immigrants to attract their hostility were the Chinese.

Many Chinese immigrants had come to prospect gold. However, they were also recruited by American industry to provide labor in the mines. They were sought by railroaders to build the transcontinental railroads. They did not leave when the railroads were completed. They did not emigrate when mines closed and there were no more great gold strikes. By the 1870s, Chinese immigrants were viewed by other workers as major competitors for jobs. The Asians were willing to work anywhere, under most conditions, for low wages. They often won jobs, and as a result they became victims of anti-Chinese rioting and restrictive state laws designed to protect others competing for the same jobs.

Despite feelings of hostility, despite flareups of illegal activities against immigrants, the nation survived. It survived and it continued to become more diverse in culture and language. It entered the post-Civil War period of industrial and agricultural growth as a richer nation. It was richer in variety. It was richer in spirit.

It was also richer economically. Much of its progress resulted from the contributions of the immigrants. There was plenty of room for new people. There was plenty of open land for them to settle. However, the national attitude did not always reflect this healthy condition. The fear that the latest newcomers would take jobs away from others continued.

In addition to the fear about jobs, there was worry about the ways in which new immigrants were "different from us." What had been primarily a nation of WASPs was changing. The population now included many Catholic and Jewish citizens. It counted among its citizenry Asians, freed African slaves, Germans, Swedes, Irish, and others. Most people accepted these changes. Some few were strongly opposed to the shifts in the composition of the nation's population.

Who defined what an American was? In 1880, it was those of the Protestant white majority. They did not include racial minorities in their definition. They did not want them to participate in the mainstream of American life. As a result, black, Asian, and Hispanic citizens were not considered to be "real Americans."

White Americans of European ancestry disagreed among themselves about who was an American. They considered themselves American. But they argued about who else deserved the title.

Suspicion of newcomers has been a pattern throughout the history of the U.S. Early arrivals have resented the arrival of others. Each new group has had to prove its patriotism. Some settlers have not been accepted during their lifetimes. Fortunately, all groups have eventually become accepted. You could probably locate first- or second-generation immigrants in your community who could tell you about their experiences as new Americans. Perhaps you are a first- or second-generation immigrant yourself.

NEW IMMIGRATION: 1882–1964

In 1882, another shift began in the country of origin of U.S. immigrants. Suddenly, while the number of immigrants from northern and western Europe remained relatively constant, many new immigrants

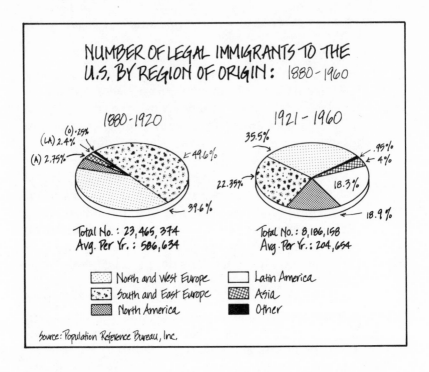

NUMBER OF LEGAL IMMIGRANTS TO THE
U.S. BY REGION OF ORIGIN: 1880-1960

1880-1920

(O) .25%
(LA) 2.4%
(A) 2.75%
49.6%
39.6%

Total No.: 23,465,374
Avg. Per Yr.: 586,634

1921-1960

35.5%
.95%
4%
22.35%
18.3%
18.9%

Total No.: 8,186,158
Avg. Per Yr.: 204,654

- North and West Europe
- South and East Europe
- North America
- Latin America
- Asia
- Other

Source: Population Reference Bureau, Inc.

began arriving from southern and eastern Europe. These settlers came in huge numbers. They were from Italy, Greece, Poland, and Russia.

At the same time, the United States Congress passed the first legislation restricting the arrival of immigrants of certain races. Thus, 1882 is the year that separates "Old Immigration" from "New Immigration."

Prior to 1882, no one had been barred from our borders because of race or religion. Because of the new law, immigration became more and more restrictive.

Restrictive legislation was passed because of two fears discussed earlier: immigrants would take jobs away from other Americans; the U.S. would no longer have a majority of white, Anglo-Saxon residents.

The specific act passed in 1882 was the Chinese Exclusion Act. It prohibited all Chinese immigration for ten years.

In 1907, the U.S. formulated an agreement with Japan. Called the **Gentlemen's Agreement,** it was a policy that called for the refusal of U.S. passports to Japanese laborers who desired to come to the U.S. While the agreement was not bound by an official law, it was binding as a matter of personal honor.

The policy of Asian exclusion from the U.S. lasted until 1943. Then China was given a token immigration quota of 105 persons per year. Restrictions against the Japanese continued until 1952. After 1952, they and other Asians desiring entry to the U.S. were brought in under a quota system. They were allowed to apply for citizenship under the quota system. However, it showed a blatant prejudice on the part of Americans, and the legislation was finally changed.

When World War I ended, attention shifted to the problem of massive immigration from Europe. The

Figure 12   The Chinese Exclusion Act of 1882 and the Gentlemen's Agreement of 1907 effectively barred all Asians from entering this country for many years.

quota act of 1921 limited immigrants from Europe to an annual three percent of the number of their foreign-born countrymen counted in the U.S. census of 1910.

The Immigration Quota Act of 1924 lowered the percentage from the quota act of 1921 to two. Also, the two percent was figured from the census of 1890, when there were few immigrants from southern and eastern Europe. The use of old statistics clearly discriminated against southern and eastern Europeans. The immigration from those areas of Europe was thus reduced under the new system.

The National Origins Provision of the 1924 legislation also limited the numbers allowed from any European country.

In 1952, Congress passed the McCarran-Walter Immigration Bill, over the veto of President Harry Truman. It continued the racist policy of the 1924 act, in general terms. However, it did allow small numbers of Asians to enter the country.

Many national leaders complained about the prejudice of U.S. immigration policy. President Eisenhower wanted to "get the bigotry out of it." President Kennedy stated that the ethnic quotas were "without basis in either logic or reason." Nevertheless, quotas based on race and ethnic background were in force until 1965, when new legislation ended the blatant prejudice.

The level of immigration continued to grow until 1914, when World War I began. Between 1882 and 1914, over 20 million people moved to the United States—the population of California is approximately 25 million. So from 1882 to 1914, almost enough people arrived to populate the entire state of California at its present level. During some years in that period, over one million people entered this country to take up permanent residence. The period marked the greatest immigration stream in U.S. history.

Immigration declined from 1914 through 1950. Two world wars, a worldwide economic depression, and restrictive legislation combined to drastically reduce immigration. Few people moved across national borders during World War I or World War II, except refugees trying to escape war. During the Great Depression of the 1930s, few people could afford to move, no matter how desperate they were to do so. Immigration legislation also kept many would-be Americans from entering the U.S.

Statistics tell the story about reduced immigration levels in a graphic manner. Between 1916 and 1950, only 8½ million persons arrived in the U.S. This contrasted with the total of 20 million who arrived between 1882 and 1916. In certain years between 1930 and 1940, more people left the U.S. than arrived here.

Immigration began to increase again in 1945, after World War II. But restrictive legislation still kept the number at a low level.

The entire period of "New Immigration" in U.S. history drew 33 million immigrants to the U.S. Thirty-three million immigrants could populate all of California with 8 million left over to settle elsewhere.

The pie charts in this chapter demonstrate major shifts in the countries of origin of immigrants who arrived during the "New Immigration" era. Before 1860, most immigrants came from northern and western Europe. Between 1861 and 1900, southern and eastern Europe sent many immigrants.

After 1921, the total number of immigrants de-

creased. Also, northern and western Europe provided more immigrants than southern and eastern Europe. Many immigrants arrived here from Canada. The shift reflects the restrictive immigration legislation discussed earlier in this chapter.

As stated, Asian immigration decreased due to restrictive legislation. However, immigration from Latin America began to increase during this period. Also, from 1950 to 1960, 300,000 Mexican immigrants arrived.

The increase in non-Anglo-Saxon residents continued to arouse strong feelings on the part of many U.S. citizens. Others were undecided about their sentiments and opinions. There were many questions about the effect of the changes in immigration. There were few firm answers.

During this same period, America was building factories. American industry needed unskilled labor. Americans also believed in the theory called **Manifest Destiny.** They believed that the United States was destined to become the greatest power in the world. In order to be the best, it needed more people to settle its empty spaces. The government wanted people to establish communities in areas from the Atlantic to the Pacific.

The desire for greater immigration was expressed profoundly by poet Emma Lazarus, the daughter of Jewish immigrants from Germany. The following lines are from her poem. "The New Colossus":

Not like the brazen giant of Greek fame,
With conquering limbs astride from land to land,
Here at our sea-washed, sunset gates shall stand
A mighty woman with a torch, whose flame

Is the imprisoned lightning, and her name
Mother of Exiles. From her beacon-hand
Glows world-wide welcome; her mild eyes command
The air-bridged harbor that twin cities frame.
"Keep, ancient lands, your storied pomp!" cries she
With silent lips. "Give me your tired, your poor,
Your huddled masses yearning to breathe free,
The wretched refuse of your teeming shore.
Send these, the homeless, tempest-tossed to me.
I lift my lamp beside the golden door!"

You probably recognize this poem about the Statue of Liberty in New York Harbor. It was chosen from among many submitted for a competition held in 1886. You can see it today, engraved on the base of the statue. It is a wonderfully sentimental invitation to prospective immigrants. When it was written, it reflected the mood of many Americans.

However, not all Americans agreed with this view of immigrants. Some thought that southern and eastern Europeans had a lower standard of morals and ethics. A select commission of Congress agreed with this prejudiced opinion.

So did anthropologist Madison Grant. He wrote:

The new immigration contained a large and increasing number of the weak, the broken and the mentally crippled of all races drawn from the lowest stratum of the Mediterranean basin and the Balkans, together with hordes of the wretched, submerged populations of the Polish ghettos . . . It is evident that in large sections of the country the native American will entirely disappear. He will not intermarry with inferior races and he cannot compete in the sweat shop and in the street trench with the newcomers.

Madison Grant's statement was racist. And it was wildly inaccurate. He used the term *race* to define ethnic groups. And of course, native-born Americans did intermarry with the immigrants from these areas. America did not suffer as a result. It benefited greatly from the mixing of these people into American society. Most Americans of the time did not agree with Grant's view. They saw his statement for what it was—an expression of fear based on ignorance and misunderstanding.

There were other prejudiced Americans. Their prejudices against immigrants were similarly based on fear. Most were not so extreme in their beliefs.

More reasonable people worried about how millions of newcomers would adapt to American society; whether or not they could and whether or not they wanted to become "American."

Some citizens believed the national character was firmly Anglo-Saxon. Therefore, newcomers were obligated to accept Anglo-Saxon customs and manners. They were also expected to give up their own customs and their native languages. Some immigrants complied to the extent that they changed their names to sound more American. For example, "Vladimir" was often changed to "Walter", "Marie" or "Maria" to "Mary." Newcomers who made similar changes tried to blend into American society. Often, they were ashamed of their foreign beginnings. They abandoned their own customs and accepted those of their new homeland.

The melting pot theory was popular then. It was the theory that each new group contributed special qualities to the nation's cultural "pot." All the qualities, or characteristics, "melted" together. In the

Figure 14   A lithograph showing a common fear among Americans of the late nineteenth and early twentieth centuries: that they would soon be outnumbered by the large numbers of immigrants who were coming to the United States during those years.

process, the meaning of the term *American* changed. No longer did it mean being just Anglo-Saxon; rather, it was a new mix of the ethnic groups that populate the U.S. Also, newcomers went through **assimilation.** Most immigrants did assimilate, or "melted into," American society. It is good that many immigrants also kept careful records of their ancestry. Thus they preserved important memories of their forefathers.

One historian commented, "The third generation remembers what the second generation forgot." This statement means that the second generation of an immigrant group was so intent on being accepted as American that it deliberately cut its ties to its homeland. The third generation, more secure about being American, looked back with pride to its heritage.

Cultural pluralism was hailed by many as the proper path for immigrants to follow. In a society practicing cultural pluralism, each ethnic group retains its distinctive identity. Each group maintains its customs and speaks its native language. While some mixing occurs, it is not encouraged. Cultural pluralism implies harmony among diverse national elements. Various cultural groups accommodate one another. There has always been some evidence of cultural pluralism in the United States. It exists in ethnic neighborhoods where native languages are spoken and native customs are practiced.

Restrictionists, people who wanted to limit immigration, were against the melting pot idea. They were opposed to cultural pluralism. President Woodrow Wilson, for example, commented, "A man who thinks of himself as belonging to a particular national group in America has not yet become an American."

Statements like this indicated that many people wanted fewer immigrants. They wanted all new immigrants to accept and practice Anglo-Saxon customs. They did not want assimilation, and they did not want cultural pluralism. They wanted the issue of immigration to disappear.

The controversy was particularly bitter at the beginning of the twentieth century. Citizens' angry feelings contributed to the passage of legislation limiting immigration on racial and ethnic grounds.

By 1965, Americans were a blend and a variety of ethnic and racial types. This was in spite of opposition to assimilation and cultural pluralism. No longer did one group dominate other groups. Persons from many ethnic backgrounds had succeeded in industry, business, education, and politics. The election of President John F. Kennedy in 1960 marked a turning point. His ancestry was Irish, and he practiced the Catholic faith. His election redefined what was acceptable in the ethnic and religious background of a U.S. president.

The Americans of the 1960s defined themselves differently, but many old prejudices remained. Black, Asian, and Native Americans were most often prevented from entering the mainstream of American culture. There were individual social, political, and economic successes, but many were kept on the fringes of American society.

However, many positive events had occurred in the decades preceding the 1960s. The beneficial impact of new immigrants was evident everywhere. A variety of ethnic groups exhibited political muscle. Italian, Greek, Polish people and others were holding public offices. Professional groups included more persons from a variety of ethnic groups.

Figure 15 Election posters showing the wide ethnic diversity of political candidates.

America had changed its idea of accepted personal style by 1960. Fashion seen on American streets reflected an awareness of clothing worn by other cultures. Americans learned about stir-frying and filling pita pockets. More pizza was eaten in the United States than in Italy. Andy Warhol, a Czechoslovakian immigrant, turned the art world upside down with his huge paintings of Campbell soup cans.

For every major impact created by a famous immigrant, there were small and subtle changes caused by countless others. The definition of an American was as varied as the persons who defined the term. Some still confined it to those persons born in the United States. Others would have said it was anyone living in the United States who wanted to be called an American.

THE NEWEST IMMIGRATION: 1965 TO THE PRESENT

By 1965, many Americans questioned the nation's laws and institutions. The Civil Rights Movement and the protests against the Vietnam War attracted the most attention. But immigration laws were also being

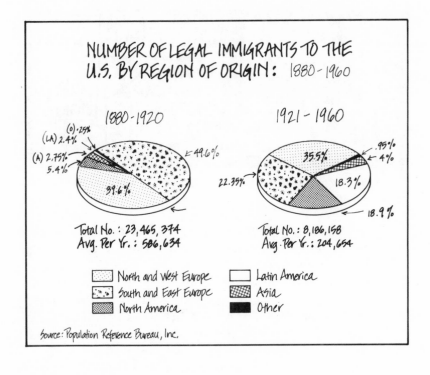

NUMBER OF LEGAL IMMIGRANTS TO THE U.S. BY REGION OF ORIGIN: 1880-1960

1880-1920

(0) .25%
(LA) 2.4%
(A) 2.75%
5.4%
49.6%
39.6%

Total No.: 23,465,374
Avg. Per Yr.: 586,634

1921-1960

.95%
4%
35.5%
22.35%
18.3%
18.9%

Total No.: 8,186,158
Avg. Per Yr.: 204,654

☐ North and West Europe   ☐ Latin America
☐ South and East Europe   ☒ Asia
▨ North America   ■ Other

Source: Population Reference Bureau, Inc.

challenged. Americans believed that the discriminatory quota system was outmoded. Citizens felt it no longer represented the nation's values or its international political goals.

Following hearings on immigration reform held during the Kennedy administration, a set of immigration amendments was signed into law in 1965 by President Lyndon Johnson. The amendments were phased into practice over a thirty-one-month period. They were in full effect by 1968. Several controversial issues arose from the changes in immigration that resulted from the new law.

The Immigration Act of 1965 represented the greatest change in immigration legislation since 1924. It abolished the practice of barring immigrants on the basis of national origins. A worldwide ceiling of two hundred seventy thousand is now in effect, with no more than twenty thousand from any single country. An important feature of the act is that there are no restrictions on the number of immediate relatives of U.S. citizens who can immigrate here. In 1980, the U.S. Congress passed the Refugee Act, which was written in order to deal separately with refugees who wanted to find a new home in America.

After passage of the 1965 legislation, America's borders were wide open to Asian immigrants. They were joined by large numbers from Latin America. Although immigrants arrived from other areas, Asia and Latin America were the major homelands of newcomers.

The 1965 law also changed the process by which legal immigrants were chosen. The Immigration Law of 1952 emphasized occupational skills as a basis for entry. The new law emphasized family reunification as a major criterion, or measurement, for deciding who would be allowed to enter. As much as three-fourths of each country's quota for immigration was allotted to close family members of U.S. citizens and to permanent resident aliens.

When the Refugee Act was passed in 1980, another six percent of quotas went to the spouses and unmarried children of permanent resident aliens. Immigration based on occupational skills was minor in comparison.

Figure 17   A woman and her child wait outside the U.S. Immigration Office at JFK Airport, 1965.

It was believed that this realignment of the quota system would result in a nondiscriminatory application of the law. By concentration on family reunification, the law helped to stabilize the families of immigrants. Stabilization of the family unit helped to stabilize immigrant communities.

The number of legal immigrants rose steadily after the 1965 amendments took full effect in 1968. However, there was also a continuation of the rise that began after World War II. In 1968, almost three hundred thousand immigrants arrived. Today, the annual immigration figure is closer to six hundred thousand. Many people think of immigration as a historical phenomenon. However, more people are immigrating to the U.S. today than have for the past fifty years.

It is fairly simple for the U.S. government to count legal immigrants. Counting illegal immigrants is a more difficult task. Illegal immigrants contribute greatly to the impact of immigration on the nation.

It is impossible to know for sure how many illegal immigrants have become permanent residents of the United States. Their legal status cannot be determined by traditional census-taking procedures. Estimates of their numbers have ranged from two to twelve million persons. Careful studies conducted by the government and by agencies in the private sector put their number at between four and six million persons.

Besides not knowing the total, the U.S. government has been unable to count the illegal immigrants who arrive in any one year. Also, many illegal immigrants return to their homeland. Many illegal immigrants come to the U.S. expecting to stay for a short time.

They plan to work for a while and return home to the families they left behind. Others are simply disappointed in the U.S. If they do not find work or are in an unhappy work situation, they may decide to leave. Being homesick causes a certain number of others to return home.

The Immigration and Naturalization Service (INS) does keep a year-by-year count of the numbers of illegal aliens apprehended at the U.S. border. Activity in 1986 indicates the scope of the problem. In that year, the INS stopped one million eight hundred thousand illegal immigrants attempting to cross into the U.S. This huge number is slightly inaccurate because many illegal immigrants try to enter more than once and are repeatedly caught. Running the risk of capture and deportation over and over again is an indication of how desperate many persons are to enter the U.S.

There is a direct relationship between the number of persons attempting illegal immigration and economic, social, or political problems in the countries they leave.

Mexico is an example with which most Americans are familiar. Its economy has been in poor condition. Mexico's currency has been devalued repeatedly, and the government has not solved its difficult unemployment problem. Mexican citizens are increasingly crossing the U.S. border. There are nightly confrontations between U.S. Border Patrol agents and Mexican citizens trying to enter the U.S. at border towns like San Ysidro, California, and Laredo, Texas. The entire U.S.-Mexico border ranges for two thousand miles. The U.S. has twenty-six hundred border agents patrolling it, or roughly one agent per mile.

The task is overwhelming. It is impossible to secure U.S. borders against illegal immigration. Hundreds of thousands of illegal immigrants succeed in slipping past border patrols every year.

Current immigration is different from past immigration in one significant way. Historically, more immigrants were from Europe than from any other continent. This is no longer true. The proportion of legal U.S. immigrants from Europe declined to just eleven percent by 1981. Conversely, the percentage of immigrants from Asia grew to forty-eight percent. Latin American countries provided another thirty-five percent of U.S. immigrants.

Among illegal immigrants, around fifty-five percent are currently from Mexico. Other Latin American countries provide another twenty-two percent. However, illegal immigrants come from many other countries, also. In 1986 the U.S. Border Patrol stopped illegal entrants from ninety-three countries.

Most of the legal and illegal immigrants who enter the U.S. have left their countries of origin because of unpleasant conditions. This fact explains why fewer

Figure 18   Illegal aliens attempt to sneak across the border and into the United States.

Japanese nationals immigrate to the U.S. than do Asians from other countries. Japan is a highly developed nation. Its citizens enjoy many opportunities; they have a high standard of living. America is a land of opportunity that looms in the future for people who are less fortunate than the Japanese. Leading desperate lives, they take desperate measures. They turn their backs on familiar surroundings and set out to resettle elsewhere. The United States is increasingly the country of choice for hundreds of thousands of would-be immigrants.

Immigration shaped American culture from our country's beginnings. New U.S. citizens from virtually every country in the world colored the way Americans speak, dress, and conduct their daily lives. Every aspect of American society has changed as the direct result of immigration.

It is impossible to identify all of the influences immigration has had on the way Americans live today, because the blend and mix of those influences has resulted in a peculiarly American style. Americans consume literally tons of hot dogs (Germany); they sometimes smother the hot dogs in chili (Mexico). Americans stuff the pita pockets they have adopted from Mideastern culture with some ingredients that persons from that part of the world have never tasted. Many common American surnames are variations on the originals: Smith (Smythe), Miller (Mueller), Greenfield (Gruenveldt), and so forth. The recent history of American immigration suggests that the American lifestyle will soon reflect more of the influence of the Asian and Latin American immigrants.

Current immigration is a topic that generates debate in the public and private sectors. Government forums, the U.S. Congress, panels sponsored by non-governmental agencies—all discuss immigration. You have talked about it at school; perhaps you debate the subject with your family and friends. The next chapter outlines some of the issues that surround current immigration practices in the United States.

REVIEW QUESTIONS:

1. Where did most of the colonists who arrived before the Revolutionary War come from?
2. What is the difference between "Old" and "New" Immigration?
3. Why is the year 1882 important in United States immigration history?
4. Who was Emma Lazarus?
5. What was the major change in country of origin that occurred between 1860 and 1920?
6. What were the "quota laws?"
7. During what period did the most immigrants come to the U.S.? Why?
8. During what period did the fewest immigrants come to the U.S.? Why?
9. Why was the Immigration Act of 1965 so important?

3 | **Contemporary Debate**

What are the current social and cultural issues surrounding immigration?

What are the current economic and employment issues related to immigration?

What is the Immigration Act of 1986, and how will it affect future immigration?

What are the current issues related to illegal immigrants and refugees?

The recent dramatic increase in immigration raises many issues. Some of these same issues worried Americans in the last great wave of immigration, in the early 1900s. There is the same fear of social and cultural change caused by newcomers. Again, many Americans worry that new immigrants will take jobs away from them or will work for less money than other American workers.

New issues have also arisen as a result of the recent immigration of people to the U.S. People worry about illegal immigrants, refugees, and the effects of the Immigration Act of 1986. Many Americans wonder how the cultures of so many different societies will blend into our own culture. Will you change? Will the new immigrants adapt to this nation's political and social systems?

These issues are important to each of you as students now and as adults of the future. This chapter examines these issues from a cultural and economic point of view. It looks closely at illegal immigration and refugee movements. Finally, it examines the immigration legislation of 1986 to see how it will affect legal and illegal immigration.

SOCIAL AND CULTURAL ADAPTATION

Should tomorrow's immigrants become like the "rest of us"? Or should they keep their own cultural identity? In the first place, the "rest of us" are a mix of races and cultures. Most Americans are not exactly like the English, nor the French, nor the Vietnamese, nor the Native Americans. Americans are a mixture of all of them, and of dozens of other races and cultures. America is a *pluralistic* society.

Secondly, many of you have two opinions. You have some fears about people who are not like you. Yet you probably enjoy the results of having new immigrants. If you live in an urban area you probably enjoy street fairs, celebrations, and food festivals hosted by immigrants. It is almost impossible to walk a mile in any major U.S. city without seeing more than one restaurant that serves the food of another country. Foreign movies are popular in the U.S.; many Hollywood filmmakers are immigrants from elsewhere, like Milos Forman of Czechoslovakia. Americans enjoy reggae music and dance to a Latin beat. There are also many other, more subtle influences on American life.

And what about the immigrants themselves? Some want to change. Some want to become assimilated into American society. They do not want to stand out from other Americans. Still others prefer to keep their cultural customs, to be different in this western democracy they have chosen as their new home.

The concerns about how well immigrants adapt to their new home in the U.S. are often echoes of concerns Americans voiced one hundred years ago. However, popular theories of a century ago about adaptation are not popular today.

Old theories about **adaptation** were based on the fact that immigrants of one hundred years ago were mostly from Europe. They were similar in race and culture to most other Americans. Today, many immigrants are non-European and nonwhite. They arrive here from cultures very different from that of the United States.

There are differences between the immigrants of 1900 and those of today. At the turn of the century, most immigrants were white. The entire population of the United States was under one hundred million. Immigrants of the late nineteenth and early twentieth centuries did speak languages foreign to our ears. However, they wanted their children and grandchildren to fit in with other Americans. Their goal was total assimilation into American society. The sons, daughters, and grandchildren of these newcomers learned English.

Many second- and third-generation immigrants grew up to become stars of American society. Michael Dukakis, the son of Greek immigrants, became gov-

Figure 19   New immigrants learning English in New York City, circa 1910.

ernor of Massachusetts and a Democratic presidential candidate. Lee Iacocca, of Italian parentage, became one of the most successful businessmen in United States history.

The quota laws of the 1920s suddenly limited the number of immigrants to the U.S. In the 1930s, the U.S. and the world experienced a brutal economic depression, which also limited immigration. Then World War II disrupted the flow of people to the U.S. And since only small numbers of people arrived from any one place, individual immigrants had time and the incentive to adopt the ways of their new home. They did not find huge neighborhoods, or ghettos, of their native countrymen when they arrived, so they became "Americanized" more quickly.

Many immigrants of today arrive to find thousands, even hundreds of thousands, of fellow immigrants. These people tend to group together in U.S. cities. They form separate societies, individual patches within the larger fabric that is U.S. society. These immigrants have less incentive to adopt the customs and language of the United States.

One outcome of this lack of interest in becoming "American" is the resistance many Hispanics have to learning English. A recent survey by Yankelovich, Skelly, and White resulted in the conclusion that "there is a significant increase in the desire to perpetuate Hispanic traditions through succeeding generations. There is no sign of increased commitment to mastery of English at the possible expense of Spanish. The commitment to Spanish is stronger, if anything."

This commitment to their cultural heritage has not kept Hispanics from succeeding in visible ways. In 1986, Florida elected its first Hispanic governor. Denver, Miami, and San Antonio all have elected Hispanic mayors. So the concern of some Americans over the resistance of some Hispanics to learning English will probably disappear as more Spanish-speaking immigrants take active roles in U.S. society. Throughout U. S. history, this phenomenon has occurred with other groups.

Asian immigrants tend to speak some English on their arrival in the U. S. This may be the result of our heavy economic and political involvement with countries like Japan, Korea, and Vietnam. In the 1980 U. S. census, over half of the recent Korean, Chinese,

Figure 20 Cuban businessmen pose in front of their successful boat building business in Miami, 1966.

and Vietnamese immigrants reported that they spoke English fairly well.

U. S. citizenship is one measure of how well immigrants adapt to U. S. society. Since each citizen has the right to vote, the exercise of that privilege indicates a desire to participate in government. It shows a willingness to help make government work for the good of all citizens. Over half of all foreign-born residents of the United States are naturalized citizens. The United States does not recognize dual citizenship. You may not be a citizen of the United States at the same time that you are a citizen of another country. So each of these residents has willingly given up citizenship in the country of their birth in order to become an American citizen. This is **naturalization.**

Immigrants from Asia are more likely to seek citizenship than those from Latin America or Mexico. Chinese, Japanese, Filipino, Korean, and Indian residents have high rates of naturalization. Only twenty-nine percent of Latin Americans living in the U.S. have become citizens. The average rate of naturalization for Mexicans living in the United States is just one-tenth that of other groups. Often this is due to circumstances the immigrants themselves cannot control.

Many Mexican residents of the U. S. are illegal immigrants. Often they plan to return home to families they left behind. Since Mexico borders the southern United States, this is a reasonable expectation for many of them. Poor economic conditions in their own country have driven them north, across the U. S. border.

This is the current situation. It will be interesting to see future profiles of recent refugees, immigrants from Mexico, and Southeast Asia. It will be interesting to see how many of them choose to become U. S. citizens.

If many new immigrants decide not to become "Americanized," what will be the result? If new residents continue to speak their native language and practice their native customs, what will America be like?

If this happens, America will become more and more a country of *cultural pluralism.* You can think of *cultural pluralism* as many cultures existing side by side. You are already familiar with examples of cultural pluralism.

Among your classmates there may be some of Greek or Russian descent who celebrate Easter on a different date than you do. Perhaps there are students in your school who don't celebrate Easter at all. Perhaps you don't. This is an example of cultural pluralism.

If you live or travel in the southern United States, you might eat grits, a dish made of coarsely ground grain. In Texas or the Southwest, many restaurants serve tortillas. These are examples of cultural pluralism. Some people think cultural pluralism is good; other believe it is not appropriate for the United States.

One of those who does not accept cultural pluralism is former Colorado Governor Richard Lamm.

America can accept additional immigrants, but we must be sure they become American. We can be a Joseph's coat of many nations, but we must be unified. We must have English as one of the common glues that hold us together. We should be color blind but not linguistically deaf . . . We can teach English via bilingual education, but we should take great care not to become a bilingual society.

Cruz Reynoso, the first Mexican-American judge on the California Supreme Court, believes that cultural pluralism is a good idea.

America is a political union—not a cultural, linguistic, religious, or racial union . . . Of course, we as individuals would urge all to learn English, for that is the language used by most Americans, as well as the language of the marketplace. But we should no more demand English-language skills for citizenship than we should demand uniformity of religion. That a person wants to become a citizen and will make a good citizen is more than enough.

Other opinions fall somewhere in the middle. You probably have an opinion on this issue, and it is probably the result of your cultural background, conversations in your home, and talks with your friends.

Some people believe that certain minorities have not adapted as well as they might have because other people have rejected them. They say these minorities have been prevented from being successful. They have been kept out of the business arena. They have been prevented from entering politics.

Because of this rejection, minorities have developed an ethnic closeness which binds them together. This ethnic closeness means they form their own neighborhoods, where their culture, identity, and internal solidarity are preserved. In other words, the outside world has rejected them. They have created their own "world" within American society.

Many minorities do have separate communities within U.S. cities. In these enclaves, it is possible for new immigrants to thrive with little or no knowledge of the English language or a broader sense of American culture. The argument has some truth. However, most people, especially second and third generation immigrants, do become more and more like the majority of Americans.

We do have cultural pluralism in the United States. Also, many immigrants do assimilate almost completely into American society. Which will prevail?

Perhaps neither. Perhaps there will always be cultural pluralism and assimilation.

Early in this century, sociologists called America a melting pot. A better term for the U.S. today is a salad bowl. America's population is a mix and blend of ethnic and racial groups. In this salad bowl the individuals keep some of their racial and ethnic identity. They don't melt into a collective pot. Each group adds a special flavor to American society. Each enriches it. You contribute to the wonderful variety that is America.

But while there is mixing and blending, there is still ethnic variety. Cultural pluralism may be limited in practice, if not in scope. Many people will do as they do now. They speak their native language at home, but speak English at school, with friends, and on their jobs. They maintain their unique cultural heritage, but they mingle culturally in the larger U.S. society.

If you speak one language at home and another at school, you are fortunate. You benefit from the language and customs of two cultures. If you have a friend who speaks English as a second language, your life is enriched by the experience.

IMMIGRATION AND THE ECONOMY

Everyone argues about how immigration affects the economy. Everyone has an opinion. A common concern is whether immigrants take jobs away from Americans who were born here. Another is that immigrants cause lower wage rates for everyone who works.

Other people ask questions about immigrants and

the economy. Do public services for immigrants cost more than the immigrants pay back in taxes? Does the United States need immigrants to fill jobs? There are no straightforward answers to these questions. These answers are as complicated as the questions.

People have argued about immigrants and jobs for more than one hundred and fifty years. The first arguments began when the Irish arrived in the U.S. The arrival in New York of immigrants from Italy, Greece and Poland started a new debate. The debate continued when large numbers of Chinese and Japanese immigrants arrived in California. Today people engage in arguments about the illegal immigrants who pour across the Mexican-American border, and about the refugees from Southeast Asia.

Businesses that benefit from paying lower wages to immigrants want immigration to continue.

Workers and members of organized labor who see a threat to jobs or higher wages want immigration to end.

There is some evidence that immigration actually creates more jobs, and does not result in the displacement of American-born workers. New immigrant workers also make new demands for goods and services. They require food, clothing, housing, medical care—all the basics of life. Their demands for goods and services create more jobs for everyone.

Do immigrants lower the wage scale for all workers? Or do they simply perform lower-paying jobs? It is a fact that there are many low-paying jobs in industry and agriculture that immigrants perform.

Owners of large farms often hire immigrants at low wages. They hire them for hard manual labor. Some people say that if these farm operators looked across the United States for workers, and paid them higher wages, they would find willing workers in the resident population. They would no longer depend on foreign workers. Furthermore, paying higher wages would encourage farmers to mechanize. Certain experts believe that owners will continue to use immigrant workers as long as they are not forced to spend money to recruit, hire, and pay workers well. The result, the argument continues, is less technological advancement. In other words, paying low wages is cheaper than investing in equipment and methods that require fewer workers.

This argument is also used to describe certain industries. Low wages, some say, are seen as business assets. Low wages allow for bigger profits. This is one perspective of the issue. There are others. You will face the issue of the impact of immigration on jobs and wages often. You will be asked to vote for political representatives who express one opinion or another in regard to immigration. You will discuss the result of immigration policy on the American economy.

There is no final statement to make about the impact of immigration on jobs and wages. The debate continues. The jury is still deliberating.

There is some agreement that the arrival of white collar immigrants produces more jobs for the entire country. And some research shows that immigrants who fill low-skill jobs don't affect other American workers. However, there is an impact on some individuals.

Columnist William Raspberry defined those individuals in 1986: ". . . I find it hard to believe that anybody interested in relieving unemployment

Figure 21 A Latin American architect in Miami.

among Americans, particularly American minorities, can believe that the influx of illegals suggested by 131,000 arrests in a single month does not do harm to the job prospects of America's own homeless."

Former Secretary of Labor F. Ray Marshall has an opinion similar to Mr. Raspberry's. "The relative openness of the American economy to immigration (legal and illegal) increases labor supplies relative to job growth and therefore reduces wages and perpetuates marginal low-wage jobs." There are other arguments like this, all difficult to prove or disprove. Certainly, in spite of immigration, Americans' wages have risen. Not many American workers compete for the manual labor and service jobs immigrants perform.

Further, some Americans see the possibility of

wage depression as a positive phenomenon. Proponents of low-wage, immigrant labor argue that it helps American companies fight foreign competition in the marketplace. This belief raises social and ethical issues. Does the U.S. want to preserve low-wage occupations? Do we want to encourage the return of sweatshops? A famous clothing designer was recently accused of running sweatshops in New York. Is this what we want? Evidence of similar sweatshops has surfaced in other communities, like Los Angeles. Are we comfortable with this situation as a nation? Are you? America may benefit in the short term from low-cost agricultural, hotel and restaurant services. But does the country want to create an underclass to perform these services? There must be better ways to maintain service industries without having people work for almost nothing in horrible settings. Every bad job setting is a negative reflection on U.S. society.

What do immigrants cost us as a nation? Do they take more in public services than they pay in taxes? Is the cost of their education, medical care, unemployment and retirement benefits greater than the money they contribute? One possibility suggested by the President's Economic Council of Advisors is that immigrants contribute more than they take. The council says that immigrants do not use public services much. However, the council does point out that illegal immigrants use health and education services often.

The Immigration and Naturalization Service, or INS, conducted a study in 1983. It disagreed with this conclusion. The report said that for each one million illegal aliens, the cost to government was $2.25 billion each year. The taxes paid by illegal aliens totalled just

$995 million each year. In other words, each illegal alien cost the United States about twice as much as he or she paid in taxes.

The INS study did not consider the money spent by the immigrants on food, clothing, and housing. This imbalance probably does not change much no matter how long the illegal immigrants stay in the U.S. Also, it probably affects certain cities more than others.

Legal immigrants, on the other hand, do increase their use of public services at the same time their incomes are rising. As they earn more, they pay more in taxes. There is no firm evidence about the end result.

What about immigrants and the labor shortage? Many economists fear that lessening immigration will cause a shortage of workers, because the population growth rate has been low for many years. Fewer young people will enter the work force than have in the past decades. Some economists argue that the U.S. will need foreign workers to fill out a shrinking work force.

Other economists say there will probably not be a shortage of workers. If there is, foreign workers can be invited in at the time to take up the slack. Many European countries do this. Then they ask the workers to leave, when they no longer need them.

No one is certain what will happen. Economist Vernon Briggs said, "There are all kinds of things that can happen, both on the supply and demand side. Maybe the labor supply will contract [shrink] and maybe we shall need less labor in the future."

In any case, the demand for unskilled workers may decline. America is moving fast into a marketplace based on high technology. This is true in all sections of the economy: agriculture, services, light industry, manufacturing.

A good example of high technology in industry is the use of robots. Robots can and do perform many of the simple tasks necessary to make products in factories. Laborers traditionally performed those tasks. In the future, you will have to develop skills robots cannot perform to compete successfully for a job.

However, while technology eliminates many low-skill jobs, it increases the demand for highly skilled workers. You will have an opportunity to choose a career that was not a possibility for your parents. You will have a chance at a career carved out of rapidly changing technology.

In conclusion, the labor market is changing. While it does, the economic impact of immigration on the U.S. is a source of debate. There is no doubt that the entry of aliens, legal and illegal, has an impact. Those immigrants who find jobs also have an impact. The results are mixed. They are both positive and negative. What you will decide in the future is whether the net effect is good or bad for this nation.

ILLEGAL IMMIGRANTS AND REFUGEES

Two types of immigrants are important features of today's immigration picture. They are illegal immigrants and refugees. Legislation affecting them has resulted in different treatment of each of them at different times. Communities where they settle have treated them differently, too.

Illegal immigrants arrive in the U.S. through ways

other than those defined for legal immigrants. The act of illegal immigration involves crossing a U.S. border without questioning by U.S. authorities, or with fraudulent documents. A fraudulent document is usually a false birth certificate or passport.

One way illegal immigrants arrive is simply by sneaking across the border. They travel singly or in groups, generally during the night. If they are lucky, they avoid capture by the patrols that range the border. Almost all of the illegal immigrants who are captured are stopped along the U.S.-Mexican border. It is long and difficult to patrol. It is also where the Immigration and Naturalization Service has most of its patrol force.

The decision to concentrate its force along the U.S.-Mexican border is the result of the great numbers of illegal aliens who attempt to enter this country along its length. Not all who cross are from Mexico. Many have traveled from Central America, and some have come from as far as South America and Asia. As the following case study shows, their journeys are difficult and filled with tense moments. Many of them are desperate to enter the U.S. Many of them suffer the disappointment of deportation to their country of origin.

CASE STUDY: MY VISIT TO THE BORDER

The Immigration and Naturalization Service (INS) invited me to visit the California-Mexico border with them. I immediately seized the opportunity to do so. I believed that it was time to look at the subject of illegal immigration from a social, rather than a statistical point of view. I travelled to San Ysidro, California, where I was met by INS agents. San Ysidro is the southernmost city in California; it borders on Tijuana, Baja California, which is the northernmost state in Mexico.

That night it was decided that I would be taken on a nighttime tour of the entire border. It was one of the most memorable experiences of my life.

A high steel fence separates most of California from Mexico. In certain places the geography makes that impossible; elsewhere a shallow river serves as the dividing point. The fence itself is full of holes that are large enough for an adult to crawl through. I saw many holes plugged with more steel fencing. Repairing the fence is a constant process.

One location in particular is the main starting point for the thousands of attempts at border crossing that are made every day—or rather, from twilight on through the night. That location is called the Soccer Field. People mentioned the Soccer Field to me throughout the day. I was surprised when I saw it. It had been the location of pickup soccer games, but now has neither goal posts nor seats. The field straddles the border and is in a valley surrounded by gentle slopes. People began to gather on the field in midafternoon. From the American hills, members of the Border Patrol watched closely from Jeeps and similar vehicles. At dusk the movement began. Literally thousands of men and women, boys and girls tried to sneak around the border patrols and into San Ysidro.

On the U.S. side of the border, INS agents drove through the roadless hills and valleys searching for illegal immigrants. Sometimes a vehicle shut off its lights in an effort to sneak up on people. This is a dangerous tactic and occasionally results in injury to a border crosser. Helicopters scoured the area from above, and relayed information to the patrols on the ground. Bright ultraviolet lights used to spot border crossers from thousands of yards away made the entire scene seem like part of a staged drama. But the action and suspense were real.

Every night this scene is replayed. Both sides know the rules. Many border agents have been injured in the process of apprehending dangerous illegal entrants; illegal immigrants have occasionally been harmed by certain agents. But overall, the behavior of the agents and those who are apprehended is peaceful. I commented to the agent I accompanied that the nightly drama is like a game of cat and mouse. I said, "I suppose you win some and you lose some." He replied, "No, we never win. We just try to keep the score down as much as we can."

During the evening I spent with the INS agent, I witnessed a number of apprehensions. I was impressed by the agent's courteousness and by the perfect Spanish he spoke. When he stopped someone, he asked, "Where are you going?" Usually the answer was, "To Los Angeles to get a job." He caught four teenagers who said they wanted to work for a few months and then return to Mexico. After the agent interviewed them, he made a phone call and a van arrived to take them to the detention center.

Many of those apprehended try to enter the U.S. again the next night. On my first visit to the border crossing point, I took photographs of individuals exiting the Border Patrol bus. The next day, I took a picture of a young man who had just been apprehended. When the film was developed, I discovered I had taken his photo on the first occasion, also.

The INS agent's night shift ended. We went together for coffee and sandwiches. As we walked, the INS agents were spotted by illegal immigrants. They ran into gutters, disappeared down the street, fled to caves in the hills to avoid being caught. Later, I saw some of the places in National City and San Pedro where illegals settle. I saw tin-roofed shacks that reminded me of the poorest villages of Africa; I saw starving dogs; I saw the sweatshops of Los

Figure 22: Captured illegal immigrant peering through the window of a bus returning him to Mexico.

Angeles, where illegal immigrants work under deplorable conditions for wages below the legal minimum. My weekend visit ended. I said goodbye to my INS hosts. It was an experience I will remember forever. It was an experience that taught me there are two sides to the issue of illegal immigration. Desperation is the best word to describe the plight of the would-be immigrant. With no work and no promise of work, many decide to risk crossing the border to seek a job and the stability of a steady wage. The immigrant is willing to try almost anything. He may pay someone to smuggle him across the border; he may try to sneak across the soccer field. If he succeeds, he must secure work that is demeaning and pays little. But even this small success is an improvement for the illegal immigrant. It is difficult to fault those who decide to sneak across the U.S. border.

The Border Patrol is on the other side of the issue. Most agents express sympathy and admiration for illegal immigrants. However, it is important to remember that any nation has the right to determine who shall and shall not cross its borders. The U.S. has immigration laws; they are administered by the INS. Without the Border Patrol, millions of citizens from poor and war-ravaged nations would swarm into the United States. No nation could assimilate such an onslaught.

The United States is the only advanced nation that shares a thousand-mile border with a developing nation. The INS border patrol plays a necessary role in trying to maintain order at the border; the agents receive little praise and thanks for their work. Yet, their effort is essential if the U.S. is to maintain control of its own borders.

Other immigrants enter the U.S. legally but overstay their visa time limits. Most of them find jobs, which is also illegal under the terms of a temporary nonimmigrant visa. These immigrants, called visa abusers, constitute half of all illegal immigrants in the U.S.

However they arrive, the number of illegal immigrants is high. According to the Immigration and Naturalization Service, the number is growing. The nature of this immigration is different from that of the past. Previously, most illegal immigrants were young, single males looking for work. Today, they are often entire families looking for a new home. These people increase the U.S. population, and will have a major impact on its character.

The Immigration Act of 1986 does affect illegal immigrants. However, because they avoid U.S. authorities it is impossible to know how many illegal residents are here now. No one knows how many enter the U.S. each year.

The United Nations defines "refugees" as persons

suffering persecution, or believing correctly that they will be persecuted in their own country. The persecution could be because of political opinions these people express. It could be because they belong to a social group, race, or religion. Before 1980 the United States defined refugees as only those who arrived here from Communist-dominated countries or from the Middle East.

Refugees apply from outside U.S. borders for per-

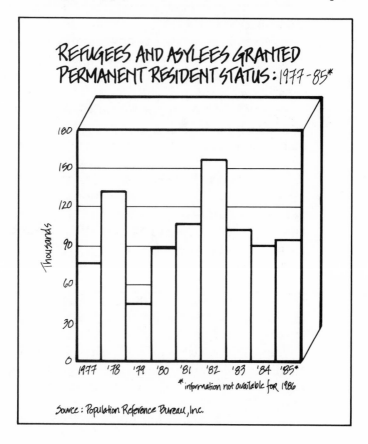

REFUGEES AND ASYLEES GRANTED PERMANENT RESIDENT STATUS: 1977-85*

Thousands

180
150
120
90
60
30
0

1977 '78 '79 '80 '81 '82 '83 '84 '85*

*information not available for 1986

Source: Population Reference Bureau, Inc.

mission to enter. They fear persecution if they return home, and this causes them to beg to stay here.

U.S. immigration law had no provision for refugees before World War II. So refugees could only enter through regular immigration procedures.

Those procedures were discriminatory. They were defined by the National Origins Act of 1924, which established quotas for immigrants based on their country of birth.

The quota system kept most refugees from entering the United States. One grim result was that hundreds of thousands of Jewish people suffering under Hitler's rule were unable to escape. Most were murdered. You have probably read stories and heard about these sufferers.

After World War II, many refugees were allowed into the United States. Ad hoc, or one-time, measures included special legislation passed by Congress. The president and attorney general also took ad hoc executive actions. For example, President Harry Truman directed that forty-five thousand displaced persons in Europe be admitted in 1945. Special legislation enacted in 1948, 1950, and 1951 allowed many more of these displaced persons to enter.

Many of these refugees, who had suffered first as prisoners of war and then as citizens without a country, became devoted to the United States. They admired the president who allowed them to enter and start life again.

There is the story of a Russian concert violinist, Vladimir Krischenko, who was allowed to settle in the U.S. with his wife as a result of President Truman's displaced-persons decree. Krischenko was so grateful that he recorded himself playing the violin.

He took the recording to Truman at his home in Independence, Missouri. The president received the violinist and presented him with a large autographed picture of himself in exchange for Krischenko's violin recording. The picture Krischenko received hung on his living room wall from that day forward.

The immigration law of 1952 did not mention refugees. However, it did establish a class of immigrants called "parolees." Parolees were aliens allowed to enter the U.S. "for emergent [sudden, unexpected] reasons or for reasons deemed strictly in the public interest."

Parolee legislation did not say how many could enter. The law was a flexible tool to use for the immigration of refugees until the Refugee Act of 1980 was passed.

The attorney general's office used parole authority to admit the refugees fleeing Hungary after the Russians put down an uprising there in 1956. When Castro seized Cuba in 1959, the attorney general's office used it again to admit the thousands of Cubans who fled the country. Most of the Indochinese refugees who fled Cambodia and Vietnam were also admitted under this special parolee status.

In 1965, refugees were given immigrant status in new legislation. Specifically, six percent of admissions to the U.S. were reserved for refugees. From then until 1980, one hundred thirty thousand refugees arrived in the U.S. because of this. The 1965 legislation saved many lives.

The U.S. Congress tried to solve the problem of refugees once and for all in 1980. They passed the Refugee Act. It broadened the definition of refugees to agree with United Nations guidelines. Instead of

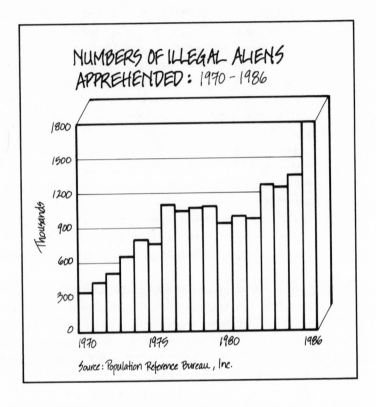

NUMBERS OF ILLEGAL ALIENS
APPREHENDED: 1970 - 1986

Thousands

1800
1500
1200
900
600
300
0

1970   1975   1980   1986

Source: Population Reference Bureau, Inc.

being tied only to immmigration quotas, the number of refugees allowed to enter the U.S. each year was also to be determined by the president, in conjunction with the U.S. Congress. Further, refugees were not allowed to become permanent residents after just one year in the U.S.

Probably no law will deal adequately with refugee immigration to the U.S. The pattern of possible refugee movements is out of the government's control.

There are about twelve to fifteen million refugees worldwide, at any given time. Most of them want to emigrate to somewhere else. Many of them want desperately to come to the United States. Refugees are the product of unstable and violent conditions around the globe. There is no way to be sure from where the next group of refugees will come.

More refugees come in some years than others. In 1960, two hundred thousand refugees were allowed into the U.S. Many of them arrived in the boatlifts from Cuba. Others came from Southeast Asia, especially Vietnam and Laos. Since 1980, the numbers have declined. There have been more refugees from certain countries, like Iran, Poland, and Ethiopia.

One single characteristic all refugees have is that they were pushed, not pulled, to emigrate from their countries. Refugees would rather stay home. They leave their homeland because they fear for their safety. They fear for their lives.

Often, the first group of refugees arriving from elsewhere is well-educated. They enjoy a high standard of living. Many of them are professional people who flee at early signs of violence or repression. This was true of Cuban refugees who came to the U.S. in the early 1960s. It was also true of the first refugees from Vietnam and Laos.

Recent Southeastern Asian refugees are farmers, fishermen, and laborers. Often they speak no English. Often they have no relatives waiting here to help them when they arrive. As a result, refugees like the Cubans who arrived during the Mariel boatlift had trouble finding jobs. When they did, they were usually low-paying occupations. For them economic and social adjustment was hard and uncertain. With

Figure 25   Vietnamese refugee girl in Falls Church, Virginia,
1978.

time, their situation improved. They learned English
as a second language. Some of them were also able
to improve their job skills. With time, the number of
them living on welfare and in poverty has declined.

The U.S. government has tried to provide refugees
with needed economic and social support. Refugee

programs include income and medical support, English lessons, employment assistance, and education.

Individual communities have helped refugees to become part of the national community. Some cities have done a better job than others.

Sometimes conflict, unrest, and hostility have erupted into violence. Longtime residents of some communities have resented the success of certain groups, like the Hmong tribesmen from the mountains of Laos, or the fishermen from Vietnamese villages. Much of the hostility here stemmed from the fact that local residents have viewed the success of these groups as a direct threat to their own economic success.

Again, time helped to end some of the bad feelings. Other communities were successful in resettling refugees. They became involved in the future well-being of these people. They helped them to understand American customs and to find jobs. The reward for these communities is the enrichment of their own culture.

The demand for refugee status in the United States changes year to year. Whether the demand increases or decreases, it will not disappear. You will face the reality of refugees throughout your adult life. Your government will continue to struggle with the question of how many refugees this nation can welcome each year. It will decide from where they should come. You can take an active part in this debate. Also, the arrival of refugees will always require planning.

Some private citizens and public officials have said that the U.S. should drastically reduce the number of refugees it allows into the country. However, historically we have always accepted refugees. The nation must weigh its ideals against the reality of the numbers and needs of modern immigrants.

Obviously, it is wrong to expect the United States to care for any and all persons who wish to live here. That has never been the policy of the government. But the decision of who to accept is difficult. The concerns about how future refugees will adapt to the United States are real.

IMMIGRATION LEGISLATION OF 1986

The growing level of illegal immigration has many Americans worried. You have probably seen television reports about illegal immigrants. It is difficult not to have sympathy for illegal immigrants. They are simply doing what others have done for centuries— moving to improve their lives. But their wish for a better life is balanced by several negative issues.

The right of the U.S. to have secure borders is challenged by the continued crossing of illegal immigrants. Further, immigrants with an illegal status invite exploitation, or misuse, by others. The existence of an economic and social subclass, which is what these people form, is unhealthy. It is unhealthy for them and it is unhealthy for the U.S. Many Americans believe that the situation is out of control. They hear that the INS has caught and deported great numbers of illegal immigrants. By 1980, most Americans believed that illegal immigration should be controlled and reduced. Most thought the immigration laws were overdue for a major overhaul.

Congressmen sponsored immigration legislation in 1982, 1983, and 1984—with no success. In 1986, the

Ninety-Ninth Congress succeeded. It passed reform legislation on immigration.

The new law made it illegal for an employer to knowingly hire an alien, or illegal immigrant, not authorized to work in the United States. Before 1986, it was illegal for an alien to enter the U.S. without proper documents. However, it was not against the law for an employer to hire that person. Even small employers of one or two immigrants are now required to verify the legal status of the people they hire.

Employers convicted of hiring violations now face civil penalties that include fines and imprisonment.

One intent of the 1986 law was to reduce the "pull" factor for illegal immigrants. This pull was the possibility of higher wages in the U.S. Employer sanctions were opposed by some Hispanic groups. They feared it would lead to discrimination against them by employers who were afraid to hire any Hispanics for fear of facing possible penalties. However, the new law established a special office to investigate any such discrimination.

Amnesty was the second issue the new law addressed. All immigrants who arrived prior to January 1, 1982, were granted temporary resident status. Each could apply for permanent resident status after eighteen months and for citizenship after five years.

The purpose of this section of the law was to recognize an obvious fact. Many illegal immigrants have lived in the United States for a long time. They have established themselves. To deport such a large groups would have been impossible. To have them stay and remain in a subclass status, was intolerable to many Americans. The immigrants were outside

Figure 26 Illegal immigrants are often paid lower than average wages. The 1986 Immigration Act, which provides for sanctions against employers of illegal aliens, should improve this situation.

the protection of the law. They lacked the sense of national community that promotes well-being.

Agricultural workers were dealt with separately in the new law. All illegal immigrants who worked at least ninety days in U.S. agriculture in 1984, 1985, and 1986 would be eligible to become temporary residents. After two years, each could become a permanent resident.

Legislators included an important feature, to answer critics who feared the new law would result in a shortage of farm workers. The provision states the government can approve the entry of replenishment workers from abroad to fill shortages of laborers. These workers would be entitled to temporary residency and, after three years, to permanent status.

What are the implications for American society of

the reform legislation passed in 1986? Opinions differ, but there is some agreement.

Those who like employer sanctions say that illegal immigration will drop. As a result, overall immigration will drop. Further, since Hispanics make up the majority of illegal immigrants, they claim the Hispanic portion of the total population will shrink. Other effects of immigration, positive and negative, will be eliminated. Southern California's job market would change radically. Its large pool of low-wage illegal workers would dry up.

Perhaps the cost of many products and services would rise. Perhaps sanctions will not prove effective over the long term. Implementation of the new guidelines could be difficult. Discrimination might become so rampant that the sanctions would be abolished.

Granting amnesty is no guarantee that all eligible illegal aliens will register for legalization. Any amnesty act is a one-time event; recent and future illegal immigrants are ineligible. They will probably form new groups of underpaid illegal residents.

The agricultural provision was probably intended to keep the situation the same. Agricultural employers still have a cheap supply of labor under the new law. Also, recently arrived illegal immigrants will be rapidly set on the road to citizenship.

In drawing conclusions about the ultimate effect of the 1986 immigration legislation, it is important to remember one fact. The law dealt only with illegal immigration. It said nothing about legal immigration. Legal immigration could rise in the long run. This would be the result of amnestied illegal aliens becoming naturalized citizens, and then requesting admission for close relatives. The entries of these relatives do not fall within the quotas.

The intent of the new immigration legislation is not to deport every illegal immigrant. The intent is to stop the increase of future illegal immigration. But it is also intended to deal humanely and realistically with America's huge population of residents without legal documents.

In the future, you may be required to show proof of resident status when applying for a job. This will be one result of the attempt to end illegal immigration. You may be affected in other ways, also. Some effects will be positive. Who knows when the next immigrant who captures our national attention will arrive? Or from where?

REVIEW QUESTIONS

1. Do immigrants take jobs away from other citizens because they are often willing to work for lower wages?
2. What are the three basic parts of the 1986 Immigration Law?
3. What is the difference between "melting pot" and "salad bowl"?
4. Where do most refugees to the United States come from?
5. How does an immigrant become a citizen of the U.S.?
6. What are the primary countries of origin of today's immigrants?

7. Name three famous Americans whose parents immigrated to the U.S.
8. Should new immigrants adapt to the ways of the U.S. or retain their own customs and culture?

4 | Future Outlook

What will the future population of the U.S. look like, and how will immigration affect it?

What cultural challenges are posed by future immigration?

What future social and economic issues may result from immigration?

What are some alternate directions for the future?

Prior chapters traced the development of immigration to the United States, from before its emergence as an independent nation to the present day. Historically, there has been a startling variety in the type of persons who come from abroad. Previous discussion focused on the impact immigration has had on this nation—culturally, socially, and economically. The last chapter discussed the country's reaction to immigration. That reaction was measured by the type of legislation passed to restrict the number and types of people who are now allowed to immigrate.

This chapter speculates on the future. Immigration will not end—not today, not tomorrow, not ever. You will face the issue of immigration, legal and illegal, many times throughout your life. What will the on-going arrival of millions of people at America's boundaries mean to you and to your nation? How will it affect your daily life as a resident of the United States?

This chapter approaches answers to these questions by taking an organized look at the future. It begins with a description of the demographics of the future. This is a picture, or profile, of the number and variety of persons in a given location. In this instance, of course, the location is the United States. Specifically, the chapter discusses how the birth rate, mortality, and immigration will all affect the population demographics of the future. It predicts the numbers and the ethnic composition of the United States of the future. The demographic section of the chapter also discusses the potential for future increases in immigration from certain countries.

Based on demographic findings, the next section of the chapter speculates, or guesses, about several issues that will face the nation as it reacts to massive shifts in the composition of its population. These issues are cultural, social, economic, and political.

The chapter concludes with an overview, or look, at different directions the nation and you might take in dealing with immigration.

POPULATION CHANGE: THE DEMOGRAPHY OF THE FUTURE

Demographics are the statistics that tell us how many and what type of people live within certain boundaries. By studying **demography** on a continuing basis, you discover what changes have occurred in your country. Specifically, the influx of large groups of people into your country not only affects you, it also affects the countries from which these people emigrated.

Immigration is not the only factor that changes a nation's population. How many children are born each year and how many persons die each year are important to U.S. demography. The birth rate and mortality rate may vary among recent groups of immigrants.

Each of you is a factor in determining future population. You will decide how many children you want to raise. Perhaps you will decide to have none; perhaps you want several children. Your decision will have an effect on future population. In a sense, you are a population actor. You will act out your decision regarding children.

The other population act everyone eventually performs is death. Whether an individual's death occurs early or late in life makes a difference to demographics. Longer life expectancy results in a larger group of elderly citizens.

Between these population acts of birth and death, most of you move at least once. You decide to move across town or across the country. This is **domestic**

Figure 27   The birth rate is one of the most important factors in determining the size of a country's population.

migration. Perhaps you will cross the U.S. border to take up residence elsewhere. Whether you are a domestic migrant or an immigrant, your moving will change the population demographics of two locations: the community you leave behind and the community where you resettle.

The **demographic behavior** of millions of people, all population actors, determines the population size and composition of the nation. Demographic behavior determines how many persons live in a particular nation. It determines how old the population is and the population's countries of origin.

Since 1972, the birth rate of American population actors has changed dramatically. Since then, American women have been averaging less than two children each. However, if two parents do not replace themselves with two children, the population eventually declines. For example, if the current birth rate (1.8 live births per woman) were maintained indefinitely, within two centuries the U.S. population would fall from 240 million to 100 million persons. Immigration, or the lack of immigration, will help to determine whether or not this dwindling of the population occurs.

The American population is living longer. You can expect to live longer, on the average, than your parents and grandparents. Americans diet and exercise more and smoke less than before. These health factors will prolong the life expectancy of your age group. Immigrants who adopt this cultural behavior will also benefit from increased life expectancy. As a result, the number of elderly citizens will increase greatly in the future.

Millions of persons outside the United States also

make decisions about their demographic behavior. They are also population actors. Today, there may be a family or an individual somewhere who is deciding to move to the United States and who will eventually live next door to you. You will be changed by this decision. The entire country is changed by these demographic decisions.

It is hard to say how many persons will move to the United States next year, or during the next ten or twenty years. Immigration laws will limit the number of immigrants, but no one knows by how much. It is possible to outline the potential for immigration in certain foreign countries. In other words, it is possible to look at who might move here and why.

One area of the world that is growing rapidly is the **Caribbean basin.** The Caribbean basin includes Mexico, Central America, the islands in the Caribbean, and the South American countries of Colombia, Venezuela, and Guyana. Over the next thirty years, the population of this area will double to 360 million people. Immigration from these countries has been large in recent years. The pressures of overcrowding will probably cause immigration from the Caribbean to continue to increase.

Further, the increase in population in these countries will be concentrated among the youth entering the **work force.** These countries already have a high unemployment rate. To accommodate the future growth rate, 35 million more jobs would have to be created before the year 2000. One economist estimated that the additional investment needed by the year 2000 just to keep the job supply from falling further behind labor supply is one trillion dollars. The country of greatest need is Mexico. This challenge is overwhelming. It is inevitable that many young workers will head north to the U.S. to seek work.

Other areas of the world, like Africa, experience periodic drought and famine. Surely many persons seeking work and a better life will attempt to immigrate to the United States from each of these nations.

As stated earlier, the falling birth rate would result in a decrease in U.S. population, except for continued immigration. Because of immigration, many persons estimate that the U.S. population, instead of declining, will grow to 300 million persons by the year 2040. What will happen, according to the best estimates of these experts, is a major shift in the ethnic composition of the population. The salad bowl of U.S. cultural and racial types will change.

In 1980, of the 226.5 million United States population, about eighty percent were white, twelve percent were black, six percent were Hispanic, and two percent were Asian. There were also very few Native Americans. If the 1986 Immigration Law is successful, net immigration could be as low as five hundred thousand per year. Nevertheless, in less than a century about fifty-nine percent of the population would consist of white residents. Hispanics would comprise sixteen percent, blacks fifteen percent, and Asians ten percent. The number of Native Americans will not change significantly.

If the new legislation aimed at eliminating illegal immigration does not work, one million immigrants could arrive each year. Then, in less than one hundred years whites will comprise less than half the population of the nation. Hispanics will be twenty-four percent, blacks fifteen percent, and Asians and

Native Americans twelve percent.

Most immigrant populations are concentrated in a few states. About two-thirds of all newly arrived immigrants settle in just five states: California, Florida, Illinois, New York, and Texas. The ethnic composition of these states and their cultural atmosphere will be affected more by immigration than, for example, Minnesota or Mississippi. By the year 2010, there will no longer be a majority ethnic group in California or Texas. Instead, every population type will be a minority: whites, blacks, Hispanics, Asians, and Native Americans. Demographic behavior, including acts of immigration, makes things happen. It changes the cultural, economic, and social makeup of a nation. The demographic behavior of millions of population actors all over the world has changed the ethnic makeup of the United States. During your lifetime, it will change more. At the same time, people are living longer. That results in another change: the average age of an American citizen will increase.

The result of the current shifts in demographic behavior is that you will constantly be redefining yourself. As Harvard University sociologist Nathan Glazer said, "The United States, it seems, is the permanently unfinished country." The challenge is exciting. You will face it throughout your lifetime. This nation is resilient. With planning and care, the changes of the future will be accommodated. The challenge will be met.

FUTURE SOCIO-CULTURAL CHALLENGES

This nation really is in the process of redefining itself. It is asking this question of itself: "What is an American?" In 1840, when many Irish and German immigrants arrived to join descendants of earlier settlers, the identity of the U.S. began to change. In 1900, when immigrants began arriving from eastern and southern Europe, the word American took on another new meaning. Every time large groups of people have come to the U.S. from the same location, some people have said they would take over the country.

Early immigrants were white Europeans. When Chinese and Japanese immigrants began to arrive in the late 1800s, they were not encouraged to invite their relatives and friends to join them. Also, millions of blacks were forced into slavery in America. However, neither Asians nor Africans were considered a part of the assimilation process. White Europeans from many ethnic groups blended and merged. Africans and Asians were effectively segregated from assimilation. Whites constituted the majority.

However, whites will not be the majority in the future. That is the major difference between the challenges of the past and those of the twenty-first century. For the first time, America faces the possibility of a society with no racial majority. Hawaii already has no racial majority. Soon California and Texas will not have one, either. No minority group will be content with second-class citizenship. Nor should they be.

The challenge facing you is larger than the challenge Americans faced a century ago. You and your fellow Americans will redefine the United States of the future. You have the opportunity to participate in the first multiracial democracy in the world.

Meeting the challenge and growing into a successful multiracial society will depend on the resolution of issues of cultural adaptation, the economy, language, and politics.

Each immigrant decides how to adapt to life in the United States. If an immigrant assimilates completely, he or she will become part of the melting pot. Partial assimilation results in more of the salad bowl plurality. However, if more migrants move into ethnic enclaves, there will be more cultural pluralism. Several cultures will live side by side, but will not interact with other groups except out of necessity. How this works will affect you. It will affect how and where you live.

The language of the future will affect you, also. Language is probably the most important indicator of the togetherness of a society. You can think of it as a glue that holds a group of people together. Today, English is the accepted language of American society. It is difficult to imagine anyone succeeding in the U.S. without some fluency in English. A society whose members cannot communicate with each other has little chance of survival. However, that does not mean that individual members of that society should not speak more than one language. As a matter of fact, bilingual citizens have the potential to be better communicators.

Some national spokespersons also believe that the U.S. should try to become a multi-lingual nation. Others believe that only English should be allowed to be spoken outside the home. Most opinions fall between these two opposing views. The issue of language is a concrete issue. It is also an emotional issue for some people.

Most people agree that it is wise for immigrants to

learn to speak, read and write the English language. It can only be helpful for each American to learn a second language. This is especially true in view of the changing ethnic nature of our population. Some of you probably already know a second language, either through studies at school or from hearing it at home.

The nation cannot delay in dealing with the language issue. Soon ethnic majorities will no longer exist in California and Texas. Soon other states, like New York and Florida, will join their ranks. A graphic example of the result of having many ethnic minorities is this: Sixty different languages are spoken by students at Hollywood High School in Los Angeles.

The situation in California demonstrates how critical the concern over language is. Of course, one solution needs no planning or programming. Students side by side in a school will talk to one another. New immigrants will learn some English. American students will learn something about other languages. Both will learn to appreciate other cultures.

Language will continue to be a concern of the future. So will the economy. The economic climate in which you live will depend partly on your input as an individual. However, it will depend to a great extent on the input of the next immigrant populations. Because of the low birth rate of Americans today, many of the new workers who enter the labor force will be immigrants or their children. After the year 2000, over ninety percent of new workers in California and Texas will be minorities: Blacks, Hispanics, or Asians. It is essential to educate this work force, especially as the U.S. moves toward an economy based on high technology.

Also, America will continue to compete with well-developed countries like Japan and Germany. The U.S. will need all of the well-qualified young workers possible to meet this challenge. The nation will want a work force with technological skills. It will want a work force skilled in languages, to communicate within and without its borders. The labor force of the future will be culturally diverse. It would be a national failure if cultural diversity were to result in a **dual economy,** where some enjoy great success and all others only experience dismal failure.

The issues just discussed—cultural adaptation, language, the economy—will all affect the political structure of the United States. Shifts in ethnic variety, a lower birth rate, a longer life expectancy—all will contribute to changes in political opinions. All will make a difference on election day, when Americans choose their representatives for local, state, and national governments.

There has always been a concern, from this nation's early beginnings, that the arrival of large groups of immigrants from nondemocratic countries would have a negative effect on the government. These fears have often been expressed. However, they have never been realized. There is no reason to believe that those fears will become reality in the future.

One outstanding result of the discussion of social, political, economic, and cultural issues is this: America will redefine itself. How it does so is important to you and to the generations that follow you. Yale University law professor Peter Schuck has put the question well: "What are we? What do we wish to become? And most fundamentally, which individuals constitute the 'we' who shall decide these questions?" Certainly you are one of the "we." You can and should take an active interest in the future of the United States.

CONCLUSION

Constant immigration to the United States is a reality. Immigrants will continue to cross the borders of your country, legally and illegally. The nation must accept this fact. Reasonable people with different opinions will have to sit together and talk to one another. They must decide how to cope with the changes continued immigration will bring to the U.S. On a personal level, you will have to cope with changes in your lifestyle as a result of immigration and the discussions surrounding it.

At the beginning of the twentieth century, when new immigrants from southern and eastern Europe were gaining in population on the White Anglo-Saxon Protestant group, some few Americans mourned the so-called "passing of the great race." Madison Grant, an anthropologist of the time, was one of those who circulated this sentiment.

Many of today's new immigrants are from Asia, Mexico, and Latin America. Again, some few Americans declare racist sentiments about these new immigrants. Most Americans, however, recognize that the United States has always benefited greatly from the influx of new people, no matter what their country of origin. Consider how much poorer the U.S. would be without the contribution of immigrants like Albert Einstein or Mikhail Baryshnikov. Famous and not-so-famous American immigrants have contributed in countless ways.

Today, you enjoy the contributions that immigrants of the past have brought to America's shores. Tomorrow, you will enjoy the input of persons who are making the decision today to emigrate from the land of their birth to the United States. This country is an attractive place to live for many reasons. One major reason is the cultural diversity brought about by the arrival of so many immigrants from so many places.

Not everyone agrees with this view. Some of your fellow citizens take the extreme view that no more immigrants should be allowed into the U.S. The Ku Klux Klan, a group that believes in the supremacy of the white race, has found in the immigrant a new scapegoat to blame for the country's social and economic ills. Other racist groups have formed armed vigilante groups to patrol the nation's borders, in order to stop illegal immigrants from entering the country. Fortunately, most Americans do not participate in the activities of these extreme groups. Nor do they agree with radical Latino groups who argue that the U.S. government should return land seized from Mexico in the War of 1846. That land now forms part of the southwestern United States.

Most Americans argue their positions in the debate on immigration based on their concerns for the immigrants themselves plus their concerns for the economic and social health of the country. Most people do not argue for an end to immigration. However, most people do disagree on the numbers of immigrants that should be allowed to settle here. Most people agree that illegal immigration should end. However, most people do disagree on how to stop illegal immigration.

One idea is clear. The nation's ethnic composition

is changing rapidly. Your country is becoming more and more diverse. This is an opportunity and a challenge. A recent article in *Time* magazine stated, "In philosophical terms, America is the world of becoming."

The process of change will continue into the twenty-first century and beyond. The process of change puts down a road that is not easy to travel. It is difficult for the immigrants, who desire to become Americans. It is difficult for citizens like you, who must help new immigrants to participate in the American dream of democracy.

Immigration will not disappear. It will not go away as a topic of discussion, either. You will hear it discussed again and again. How you deal with the subject of immigration will affect you and the immigrants. Ultimately, it will affect the nation. You probably already interact with persons of many ethnic backgrounds. You will probably continue to do so. The experience can enrich you and reward you with new friends and new understanding.

The immigration of the future will affect you in other ways. It will determine what kind of job you choose, what kind of taxes you pay and what your cultural and social life will be like. It will affect the small details of your life, like the food you eat, the clothing you wear, and the type of entertainment available to you. You will be changed by immigration in some ways too subtle to recognize.

Some of you are the descendants of immigrants who came here one or two generations ago. It doesn't really matter when you or your family arrived. It should not matter how racially or culturally mixed you are when it comes to your participation in this nation's future. You are an American, whether by birth or choice.

The cultural mix each of you contributes to helps to make the national experiment in democracy work. This nation has a history of dealing successfully with the impacts of immigration. You should be guardedly optimistic that you and your peers will deal successfully with immigration in the future.

Henry Muller, a senior editor at *Time*, said, "No other country has the courage to let its demographic mix change so quickly, and to bet that doing so will continue to enrich it." This upbeat statement is true.

Herman Melville unwittingly expressed the result of immigration on the national character of the country when he said, over a century ago, "We are not a nation, so much as a world." It is a world asking you to participate. That is your right and your privilege. It is also a responsibility you are charged with by your ancestors, no matter where they came from. It is your duty to your successors, no matter where they settle. Immigration is in the past, in the present, in the future. You are part of the future.

REVIEW QUESTIONS

1. What is the Caribbean basin?
2. What states will soon have no ethnic majorities?
3. Name three famous foreign-born Americans.
4. Should all citizens be required to learn English?
5. What are the factors that can change a nation's population?

6. How do your actions affect the population as a whole?
7. If, as some experts project, whites are no longer an ethnic majority by the year 2040, what social and political effects will this have on the U.S. population?

GLOSSARY

Adaptation   The process by which an immigrant adjusts to living in a new country.

Assimilation   A type of adaptation by immigrants. The newcomers adopt the customs and language of the United States, and in the process give up their own language and customs.

Caribbean basin   An area including Mexico, Central America, the islands of the Caribbean, Columbia, Venezuela, and Guyana. The population of this area will double in the next thirty years, and many future immigrants to the United States will come from this region.

Countries of origin   Countries from which immigrants come to settle in the U. S.

Cultural pluralism   A type of adaptation by immigrants in which each group's culture is maintained and little assimilation takes place.

Demographic behavior   The fertility, mortality, and migration patterns of people throughout the world.

Demography   The study of population; how and what kind of people live in specific regions.

Domestic migration   Migration across county or state lines within one country.

Dual economy   An economy where there are only two sectors: those employed in high-level jobs and those in lower-paying service and agricultural jobs.

Emigrant   A person who leaves his or her native country to settle permanently in a new country.

Ethnic enclaves   Areas in cities where members of certain ethnic groups reside together and retain their native customs and language.

Forced immigrants   People who are involuntarily moved from their native country to settle permanently in a new country.

Gentlemen's Agreement   An agreement between the United

States and Japan limiting the number of Japanese laborers allowed into the United States.

Illegal immigrant   A person who either enters the country without proper papers or enters the country and stays beyond the expiration date on his or her visa.

INS   The Immigration and Naturalization Service. This agency of the federal government is responsible for issuing passports and patrolling our borders to assure that no one enters illegally.

Job displacement   The process by which an immigrant takes a job away from a citizen or legal resident of the United States.

Legal immigrants   People who cross an international border with the intention of settling permanently in a new country.

Manifest Destiny   The late nineteenth-century sentiment that the United States was destined to become the largest and most powerful nation in the world.

Multilingual society   A society where many different languages are spoken and there is not necessarily one universal language. Some people fear that the United States will someday become a multilingual society if new immigrants do not learn English.

Naturalization   The process by which an immigrant becomes a citizen of the United States.

New Immigration   The flow of immigration from 1882 through 1964. The majority of immigrants during this period came from southeastern Europe.

Old Immigration   The flow of immigration from 1800 to 1882. Most of the immigrants during this period came from northwestern Europe.

Open Door Policy   The policy of unrestricted immigration that existed in the United States until 1882, when the first laws restricting immigration were passed by Congress.

Refugees   Persons suffering persecution, or with a well-founded fear of persecution because of political opinion, membership in a particular social group, race, or religion.

Restrictive legislation   Laws passed by the Congress limiting the number and the kinds of people who can immigrate to the United States.

Salad bowl   A type of cultural adaptation that is similiar to the "melting pot," but in which ethnic identity is retained.

WASP   An acronym for White Anglo-Saxon Protestant. A majority of the original settlers of the United States were WASPs.

Work force   the number of people working or looking for work at any point in time.

BIBLIOGRAPHY

Briggs, Vernon M., Jr. *Immigration Policy and the American Labor Force*. Baltimore: Johns Hopkins University Press, 1984.

Chiswick, Barry R., ed. *The Gateway: U.S. Immigration Issues and Policies*. Washington, D. C.: American Enterprise Institute, 1982.

Davis, Cary, Carl Haub, and JoAnne Willette. "U.S. Hispanics: Changing the Face of America." *Population Bulletin* 38-(No. 3).

Easterlin, Richard A., David Ward, William S. Bernard, and Reed Uoda, *Immigration*. Cambridge, MA: Belknap Press, 1982.

Ehrlich, Paul R., Loy Bilderbeck, and Anne H. Ehrlich. *The Golden Door: International Migration, Mexico and the United States*. New York: Ballantine, 1979.

Fawcett, James T., and Benjamin V. Carino, eds. *Pacific Bridges: The New Immigration from Asia and the Pacific Islands*. Staten Island, N. Y.: Center for Migration Studies, 1987.

Gardner, Robert W., Bryant Robey, and Peter C. Smith. "Asian Americans: Growth, Change, and Diversity." *Population Belletin 40 (No. 4)*.

Glazer, Nathan, ed. *Clamor at the Gates*. San Francisco: Institute for Contemporary Studies, 1985.

Hofstetter, Richard R., ed. *U.S. Immigration Policy*. Durham, N. C.: Duke University Press, 1984.

Keely, Charles. *U.S. Immigration and Refugee Policy*. Lexington, MA: Lexington Books, 1983.

Lamm, Richard D., and Gary Imhoff. *The Immigration Time Bomb*. New York: Dutton, 1985.

Muller, Thomas, and Thomas J. Espenshade. *The Fourth*

Wave: California's Newest Immigrants. Washington, D. C.: The Urban Institute, 1985.

Portes, Alejandro, and Robert L. Bach. *Latin Journey*. Berkeley, CA: University of California Press, 1985.

Reimers, David M. *Still the Golden Door: The Third World Comes to America*. New York: Columbia University Press, 1985.

Suggested Reading

Anderson, Lydia. *Immigration*. New York: Watts, 1981.

Ashabranner, Brent. *The New Americans*. New York: Dodd, Mead, 1983.

Blumenthal, Shirley. *Coming to America: Immigrants from Eastern Europe*. New York: Delacorte Press, 1981.

Eiseman, Alberta. *From Many Lands*. New York: Atheneum, 1970.

Freedman, Russell. *Immigrant Kids*. New York: Dutton, 1980.

Gerver, Susan. *Coming to North America from Mexico, Cuba and Puerto Rico*. New York: Delacorte, 1981.

Perrin, Linda. *Coming to America: Immigrants from the Far East*. New York: Delacorte, 1980.

Rips, Gladys Nadler. *Coming to America: Immigrants from Southern Europe*. New York: Delacorte, 1980.

Tripp, Eleanor B. *To America*. New York: Harcourt Brace Jovanovich, 1969.

Articles

"After Liberty Weekend". *New Republic*, July 28, 1986, 9–10.

Arditi, L. "Fugitives from Apartheid," *The Progressive*, April 1987, 32–34.

Burger, W. "New Trouble Along a Porous Border." *Newsweek*, March 17, 1986, pp 36.

Cuomo, M. "The American Dream and the Politics of Inclusion." *Psychology Today*, July 1986, 54–56.

"Dreams of a New Land." *U.S. News and World Report,* December 30, 1985–January 6, 1986, 20–21.

Edmiston, S. "1986: Year of the Woman Immigrant." *Working Woman,* July 1986, 53–56.

"The Gifts Migrants Bear." *America,* December 28, 1985, 454–455.

"Immigrants (Special Issue)." *Time,* July 8, 1985, 24–31.

"Immigration Legislation." *Congressional Digest,* March 1986.

"Immigration Under Fire (Special Issue)." *Scholastic Update,* September 6, 1985, 4–24.

Johnson, T. E. "Immigrants: New Victims." *Newsweek,* May 12, 1987, 57.

"New Faces for America." *Newsweek,* July 14, 1986, 30–31.

Martz, L. "The Forgotten Immigrants." *Newsweek,* July 14, 1986, 32.

"Promise of America (Special Section)." *U.S. News and World Report,* July 7, 1986, 25–35.

Recio, M. E. "Tiptoeing through the Immigration Minefield." *Business Week,* March 31, 1986, 41.

Sheehy, G. "The Victorious Personality: Cambodian Refugee Phat Mohm." *New York Times Magazine,* April 20, 1986, 24–27.

Stengel, R. "Out of the Shadows." *Time,* May 4, 1987, 14–17.

"U.S. Denial of Political Asylum to Certain Central American Peoples: Notes and Comment." *New Yorker,* July 28, 1986, 17–18.

Whitman, D. "A Chance to Leave the Sweetshop Behind." *U.S. News and World Report,* May 11, 1987, 18.

INDEX